Corporate Uncertainty & Risk Management

by Edward P. Lalley

Published by Risk Management Society
Publishing, Inc., New York, an affiliate
of Risk and Insurance Management Society, Inc.

Printed in the United States of America.

Library of Congress Catalog Number: 82-060961
ISBN 0-937802-03-4

About the Author

Edward P. Lalley is President and Chief Executive Officer of Ideal Mutual Insurance Company, the Optimum Companies and Ideal Insurance Company Ltd. (Bermuda). He holds a BS degree from St. Ambrose College and an LLB from the University of Tulsa School of Law.

Mr. Lalley began his insurance career as Director of Insurance and Claims with American Airlines. In 1959, he joined Kraft, Inc. as Insurance Manager. He was elected President of Ideal in 1963.

Mr. Lalley is the author of articles on Captive Insurance Companies and Self Insurance Programs and similar subjects.

In addition to being an elector to the Insurance Hall of Fame, Mr. Lalley is the Vice Chairman of the Corporate Insurance and Reinsurance Company Limited (CIRCL) and Treasurer of the Captive Insurance Companies Association (CICA). He was recently reelected to a second term as President of the New York State Mutual Insurance Association (NYSMIA).

Acknowledgments

To all of the people of the Risk and Insurance Management Society, and particularly Ron Judd, Dan Sullivan, Ed Lloyd, Dick Hackenburg, Dick Soper, Allan Goldberg, and especially Rita Epstein (the mighty whip), who lent moral and functional support toward the successful accomplishment of this project.

To Duane Allen, Miles Chenault, Tom Duffield, Jim Mascarella, Frank McCahill and Bob Reeves, who are all keen students of the practice of risk management, and who read and critiqued this text, thus enhancing its value.

To Katie Donovan, Darlene Gentry, Craig Kalck, Joanie Mezlis, Ronnie McCarthy, Arthur York and all the other members of the Ideal Mutual organization. To say this book would not have been written without them is not false modesty, but grim reality.

To John Richman, Chairman and Chief Executive Officer of Dart & Kraft, Inc., both personally and as a representative of the employees of Kraft, Inc., a group of very nice people with whom I was associated for 13 happy years.

Elsewhere I have acknowledged the debt to my wife and our three children. Not to acknowledge a similar debt to my brothers and sisters—all seven of them—would be a serious omission.

This book is dedicated to my wife, Mary, and
our three children, Kathy, Jean and Ned.

Contents

1

Risk Management—What Is It?

In recent years a new title—risk manager—has begun to appear on the organization charts of more and more corporations. At least one-third of the largest corporations have converted from "insurance manager" to "risk manager."

Why the trend? What does it mean? It is not the result of an exploding new technology and the consequent need for new specialization, as has been the case with such new specializations as "computer programmer" or "telecommunications manager." Instead, the trend to "risk manager" stems from two interrelated concepts which have been emerging in large corporations:

- The realization that the corporation is subject to a host of risks which can be analyzed, evaluated and protected against, so that the corporation will not suffer embarrassing or crippling losses.
- The gradually diminishing role played by the insurance industry in the treatment and the ultimate disposition of risks.

The Nature of Risk

What is risk? There are many definitions. One definition from the academic world defines risk as "the possibility that a sentient entity will incur loss."[1] According to the Dictionary of Insurance Terms of the Chamber of Commerce of the United States, risk is simply the "chance of loss." But virtually every event in nature contains some chance of loss. So, to adopt such a broad definition would dump into the lap of the risk manager a responsibility for some aspect of practically every happening in the corporation. The risk manager would be stepping on the toes of most of the other managers in the company, including the chief executive officer.

So, how do we define the spectrum of risks that rightfully come

---

[1] Ron Horn and Robert Crowe, as reported by Professor Charles P. Hall in the *Journal of Risk and Insurance,* September, 1967, p. 462.

within the purview of the risk manager? Some say the risk manager's realm is the "static" risks of an organization, as opposed to the "business" risks. Static risks are those possibilities of loss which the corporation cannot avoid. Like death and taxes, they are always with us. Business risks are defined as those a business can elect to take or not take and which contain the possibility of gain as well as loss.

An example of a business risk might be the risk that a company sales program will not meet its objectives, with consequent financial loss to the company. Or, it might succeed beyond all expectations.

Another differentiation is between "pure" risks and "speculative" risks. Pure risks are generally defined as similar to static risks, but with particular emphasis on the loss-no-gain possibility. Speculative risks are generally defined very much like business risks. Although "speculative" may imply gambling, it better describes the concept and so is preferable to the term "business."

Insurable Risks

Still another term used to describe those risks the risk manager should assume is "insurable" risks. This assumes those risks not within a risk manager's purview to be speculative risks (or business risks).

At least one billion dollar company uses the title "insurable risk manager." But this definition of the function seems much too limiting. It reduces the scope of the responsibility again to that of an insurance manager.

However we define risk, we do see evidence of a significant change in emphasis in the function. No longer is it limited to an automatic transferral of corporate risks to an insurance company.

The nuance implied by the title of risk manager is that, while the person must successfully ascertain, analyze and ameliorate corporate risks, the risks need not necessarily be placed with an insurance company.

Fortuitous vs. Calculated Risks

I believe that Joseph T. Parrett, former Carnation Company risk manager, now retired, did the best job to date of delineating the two categories of risk. Writing in the *Insurance Buyers Guide* in December, 1969, he described the risk manager's job as one of handling mainly the "fortuitous" risks, as contrasted to "calculated business" risks, for which the risk manager has, at most, only limited responsibility. He said:

"If we do not attempt to be too definitive and split hairs, we can regard a risk as being that situation where a firm could sustain an out-of-pocket loss as the result of an occurrence or development. The risk could be relatively major or minor. The risk manager's job is to discover and identify those risks and then evaluate them to determine whether they are major or minor.

"The risk manager's activities as presently defined in most firms do not encompass dealing with all types of risks, particularly the so-called calculated business risks such as losses from extension of credit, investments, unprofitable operations, bad judgment, etc. The management of most firms look to their risk manager to control or eliminate those risks directly involved with fortuitous events. There are some gray areas between the fortuitous and normal calculated exposures that can often involve the risk manager."

This delineation and description has not been widely used. And it seems not to have been accepted at all by the academicians. One insurance professor calls our attention to the fact that the purest of "pure" risks (loss of one's house by fire, for example) becomes a "speculative" risk to the insurer electing to insure it. Other students of the subject emphasize that the corporate risk manager is involved only in "fundamental" risks and define these as possibilities of loss to which whole classes of people or enterprises are subject, more or less uniformly, as distinguished from "particular" or "personal" risks which are not so widely distributed.

Death is Fundamental

The risk of premature death is probably the most fundamental of risks, followed closely by accidental injury or disability due to disease. Examples of personal and particular risks are losing one's job, expulsion from one's professional society or being charged with criminal misconduct. Note that personal or particular risks are more readily controllable by the individual than are the fundamental risks.

This emphasis on fundamental risks in the study of corporate risk management is understandable. For a risk to be transferred to an insurer, enough persons must be subjected to the risk with enough regularity to make the shifting feasible.

A television comedian described his wife's insurance program as providing huge indemnity at miniscule cost for the accidental death of a family member by being trampled to death by a pregnant giraffe in the family living room. The humor stems from the ridiculous. Too few people are subjected to such a risk to make it feasible to shift or transfer it.

At the other extreme, a 100-year-old man, no matter how healthy, cannot buy insurance against death. The 120,000 people in the United States who attain their 99th birthday this year will, actuarially speaking, die before reaching their hundredth. Again, actuarially speaking, we are dealing here with certainty and not uncertainty.

The Joker

One of the best descriptions I have heard of corporate risk management came from a top management member of a large corporation. After listening to various efforts to define the corporate risk manager's area of concern, he came up with the following description:

"We're talking about the accidental risk to which the corporation is subject, rather than the calculated risk, right? Aren't we then talking about the 'joker' which exists in practically all situations of any importance—the unexpected loss? It is completely unrelated to those risks which are intrinsic to the subject at hand and which the person in charge of the operation, be it plant manager, shop foreman or sales promotion manager, is not likely to focus on unless reminded to do so."

Let us examine this concept further. Typical plant managers are faced with daily problems of raw materials procurement, the proper use and operation of plant machinery and the recruiting of the right kind and number of people. Persons so engaged are probably not going to think consciously very often about the risk of the plant being destroyed by fire unless it is called to their attention. Other problems, which occur almost daily, crowd into the consciousness and tend to crowd out attention to the risks that have less immediacy.

Don't Blame the Shop Foreman

The accidental risks are remote—not likely to happen at this particular time and with no obvious physical portents or premonitions to suggest dramatically that they will occur. Similarly, the shop foreman, with the working day filled to overflowing with the problems of manpower utilization, material and machine usage, is certainly not to be blamed if the remote possibility of injury to employees by industrial accident is not uppermost in his mind.

Nor should the sales promotion manager, beset with difficult problems of how well the sales message will persuade the public to buy the product, be expected to become concerned with the remote risk that the billboard used to broadcast the message will be blown over in a windstorm. These accidental risks are among those that are the concern of the corporate risk manager.

Management would find risk management easier to understand if practitioners would emphasize that they deal in "accidental risks" and that the "calculated" or "predictable" risks are beyond their realm. Although this term contains redundancy, its use could make risk managers better understood.

Perhaps the best of all semantical worlds would be for the term risk to mean only what we now describe as pure or static or insurable or fundamental risks; and use the term venture to describe what we now call business or speculative risks. The term venture capital tends to strengthen this concept. Of interest here is a giant worldwide oil company which has appointed a corporate vice president of international ventures.

Improved understanding of risk management by top corporate management could pay huge dividends. People are reluctant to support that which they don't understand. To achieve its full potential in the corporate environment, the risk management function has to gain the understanding of all ranks of management, and particularly of top management.

Exchanging Small Loss for Large

One thoughtful student of risk management has described insurance as a procedure whereby the insured voluntarily accepts a small, certain loss (the premium) in exchange for being freed from the payment of a larger, though uncertain, loss if it occurs. Since corporate risk management is an enlargement of corporate insurance management, this definition sets forth the risk management function very well.

As for the "small, certain loss," the corporation need not necessarily pay a premium to an insurer. The "small, certain loss" might well be applied to install equipment to diminish the chances that the loss would occur. Or the corporate risk management department might recommend that the risk be self insured—that a small part of the corporation's current profits be periodically credited to a reserve maintained on the company's books.

Spreads Loss Over Time

This procedure spreads the cost of unusually large losses over several years, thus achieving the same effect as if the risk were handed to an insurance company. In this manner, a large loss can be absorbed without financial embarrassment to the company.

This procedure has been called vertical absorption of loss, in contrast to horizontal absorption of loss when an insurance company is used as an intermediary to pool the premiums to cover losses of many corporations (or individuals).

This do-it-yourself device of self insurance has been further refined by the establishment of captive insurance companies.

Both vertical and horizontal absorption of risk can be used at the same time and on the same risk. The most explicit example is found in life insurance.

Vertical and Horizontal

When I was 16, my father bought me an ordinary life insurance policy with a face value of $1,000. It was the "cash value" type which accumulates part of the premium paid in the early years of the policy into a fund called cash surrender value, which can be used for several purposes.

More often than not it is emphasized that this fund acts as an equalizer which, when added to the true risk charge (which increases as the insured person gets older), makes the premium paid an equal amount throughout the lifetime of the insured person.

Not so often emphasized is the fact that this fund acts to reduce the amount which the insurance company has at risk. So, 20 years after the inception of my life insurance policy, the cash surrender value was about $450, built up at the rate of $30 of annual premium plus the interest accumulated through the years.

Even the experts disagree over the legal status of this cash surrender value fund—about who actually owns it, the insurer or the insured. At least it is still in the possession of the insurer. Under any theory of ownership, it would appear irrefutable that the insurer who issued the policy had $550 at risk after 20 years and not $1,000, the face value of the policy.

Obviously the build-up of the cash surrender value fund throughout the years is a vertical absorption of a portion of the $1,000 which would have been paid out in the event of early death which is, of course, the accidental risk inherent in all life insurance policies.

The remaining $550 of the face value of the policy is still being spread by the insurer among the people who have pooled the risk of untimely death through the insuring process. So it is also a good example of horizontal absorption of risk.

No such vertical integration is available in any program or policy of any conventional property-liability insurance company. Some aspects of vertical integration are involved in the calculation of premium by the use of past loss data of the individual corporate insured to develop future premium costs. But there is nothing as formalized as in the case of a cash value life insurance policy. Perhaps it is because of this that the vertical absorption of risk principle came into being in self insurance and captive insurance programs.

Manageable Risks

One student of the subject has said that the corporate risk management department should concern itself with "manageable" risks which arise solely out of the activities of the firm and are incidental to them; are associated with the occurrence of an undesirable contingency that can only produce economic loss; and are identifiable and both the frequency and the severity are to some extent subject to probability estimates.

Interlocking Functions

In corporations today, responsibilities of most managers are diffused among two or more specialties. Risk management is no exception.

Because of this diffusion, chart makers have begun to depict the corporate organizational structure by drawing a series of interconnecting circles, rather than the traditional boxes connected by vertical and horizontal lines.

Using the newer device of interlocking circles, the typical risk management function in a large corporation looks something like this.

POSITION CHART
RISK MANAGEMENT DEPARTMENT
__________ CORPORATION

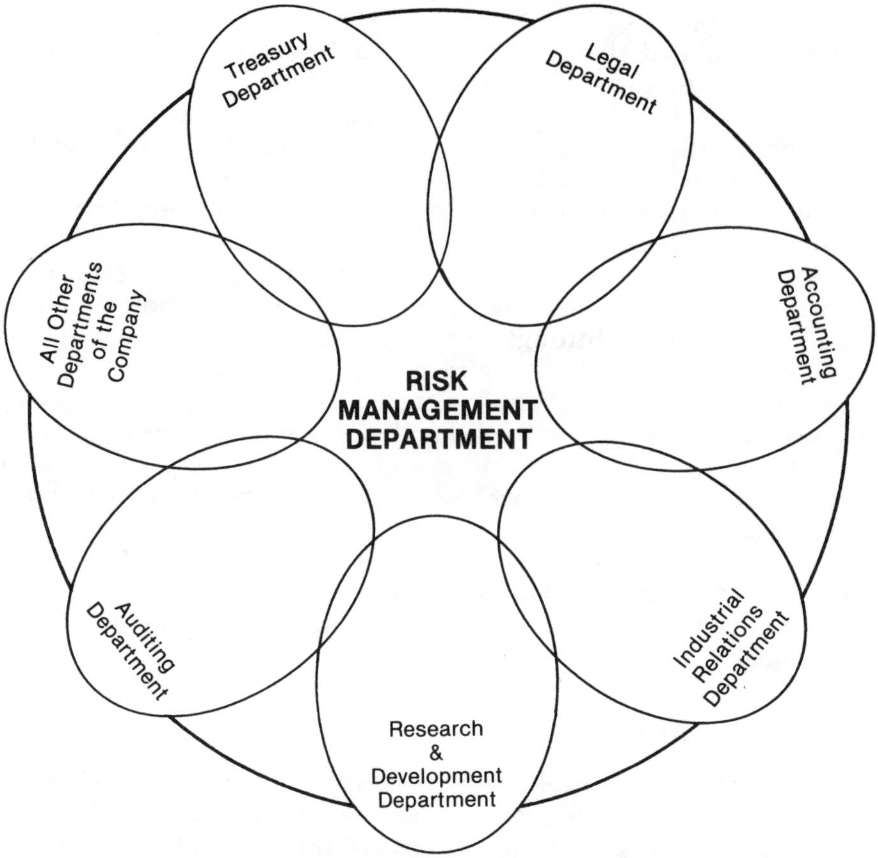

FUNCTIONS OF RISK MANAGEMENT DEPARTMENT

1. Assists all company departments to determine "fortuitous" risks. Works with those departments to develop ways to minimize these risks. Recommends whether to insure, self insure or retain those risks. Obtains and evaluates insurance rates where necessary. Helps departments develop data needed for compiling insurance or self-insurance rates.

2. Reports to treasurer. Reviews risk management program with treasurer to help keep top management advised of the program. Helps treasury department to develop cash flow and cash requirement charts on risk management expenditures, including corporate insurance premiums.

3. Assists legal department to review all contracts which might increase fortuitous risks of the corporation. Makes appropriate recommendations to minimize or stabilize these risks.

4. Assists accounting department to develop the proper accounting entries involving the corporate insurance and self-insurance programs.

5. Coordinates all workers' compensation and insured employee benefit payments with the industrial relations department. Helps this department develop data for negotiating with unions.

6. Assists research and development department to determine the extent, if any, of fortuitous risks in new product design. Advises the department promptly of any incidents of claims which might relate or pertain to this area.

7. Assists auditing department to administer the employee fidelity bond program.

2

A Word About Words

This chapter presents a series of definitions of terms we use throughout this text.

Risk

Let's start with a key word—*risk. Risk* is the chance or possibility of loss. Closely associated with it are two other terms, *peril* and *hazard.* A *peril* is the agency, such as fire, windstorm, or flood, which actually causes a loss. *Hazard* describes those conditions which enhance the possibility of loss. Thus a pile of oily rags in your garage is a *hazard,* the existence of which enhances the possibility that the *peril* of fire will occur, thus increasing your *risk* of loss by *fire.*

Accident, Occurrence, Event

If your garage does start burning, you have suffered an *accident* which is a sudden, unintended happening generally resulting in injury to a person, or damage to property, or both. The term *accident* is also a key one in any text on risk, since an *accident* is a risk which has occurred. The term *accident* is often grouped with two other terms, *occurrence* and *event.* An *accident* is a sudden, one-time happening. An *occurrence,* however, can be a series of happenings spread over a period of time. Thus if you are insured on an *occurrence basis* rather than on an *accident basis,* you are more greatly protected. The term *event,* when used in an insuring clause, provides broader protection than that provided by the term *accident* or *occurrence.* From an insurance point of view, an *event* is a series of accidental happenings all having the same cause. Thus, a hurricane is an *event* made up of numerous *accidents,* each of which involve destruction or damage. This distinction is often significant to the corporate insured which might have buildings or other facilities widely dispersed yet susceptible to damage from one *event,* such as a hurricane.

Insurance

Let us now examine what is meant by *insurance, insurer, insured, the insured,* and other terms often used in conjunction or interchangeably with these terms.

Insurance in its broadest sense is a key term in any risk management study. It is also a term which stimulates many definitions and descriptions. First take the legal definition from Black's Legal Dictionary:

"A contract whereby, for a stipulated consideration, one party undertakes to compensate the other for loss on a specified subject by specified perils. The party agreeing to make the compensation is usually called the 'insurer' or 'underwriter'; the other, the 'insured' or 'assured'; the agreed consideration, the 'premium'; the written contract, a 'policy'; the events insured against, 'risks' or 'perils'; and the subject, right, or interest to be protected, the 'insurable interest.' "

In the Random House dictionary we find that insurance is "the act, system, or business of guaranteeing against loss or harm."

An insurance dictionary defines insurance as a ". . . contract . . . whereby . . . the insurer agrees to pay an agreed amount of money to the insured if and when the latter may suffer some loss or may be injured by some event, the happening of which is described in the contract . . ."[1]

A philosophical definition of insurance is "the accumulation of small amounts from the many who are subject to the loss, to pay for the losses of the few who do suffer the loss" (author unknown). Another unknown source describes insurance as "the payment of a small but certain loss (the premium) in return for indemnification for a larger although uncertain loss if it occurs." Of the hundreds of other definitions of insurance, I prefer this: "Insurance is the pooling of risks on a voluntary basis through the use of intermediaries."

Emphasis on the pooling aspect of insurance was probably first made by Dr. Ralph H. Blanchard in 1949 in the U.S. Chamber of Commerce's Dictionary of Insurance Terms, with the preferred definition of insurance as "a pooling of hazards in order to indemnify those who experience losses."

---

[1] Gallagher and Heath, *Insurance Words and Their Meaning.* The Rough Notes Co., Inc.

For fun, we might add the corrosive definition from Ambrose Bierce's *The Devil's Dictionary:* "Insurance is an ingenious modern game of chance in which the player is permitted to enjoy the comfortable conviction that he is beating the man who keeps the table."

Insurers

With rare unanimity all students and practitioners of the subject agree that the provider of the insuring service should be called the *insurer.* For reasons neither logical nor clear, some practitioners refer to insurers as *carriers.* It would be beneficial both to the insurance industry and to the transportation industry if the term *carrier* were reserved for transporters of goods.

In an incisive speech to the Insurance Advertising Conference, E. B. Weiss, vice president, Creative Merchandising, a New York based advertising agency, had this to say of the word *carrier* for an *insurer:*

"If ever an industry proclaimed its lack of understanding of modern society and modern marketing, the continued use of the traditional term 'carrier' by the insurance industry *spells this out.* Originally, the function was indeed 'carrier.' The carrier decided the forms of protection it would make available—and then carried the risks. This was very largely what consumer goods manufacturers did before the age of modern marketing. They decided what the factory would make—and that was what the public had to take.

"But modern marketing starts with what a constantly changing public wants—and then caters to those wants. That requires an *organization committed to innovation* and to modern marketing—which is quite rare in insurance. That commitment also includes sophisticated market research on a large scale—a function that also remains elementary in insurance. These lacks may explain the industry's current image which is probably more unattractive than at any time since the Hughes investigation at the turn of the century."

The Insured

The preferred term for the party receiving the protection afforded, is *the insured.*

Much clarity in insurance semantics was lost because insurance was not a specific subject for litigation in the early common law courts of England after the Norman invasion. If it had, this second party to the insurance contract would probably be known as the *insuree.* The Norman-French passive participle was retained in the language of the emerging law court system thus providing the distinctive suffix "ee" to describe the parties to whom promises were made (promisee), land was deeded (grantee), gifts were given (donee).

The term, *the insured* to designate the acceptor of the service is probably a shortened version of *the insured party.* Since the word "insured" can also be used as the past tense of the verb, practitioners probably became uneasy with sentences that included "the insured was insured," and the insidious habit of referring to *the insured* as *the assured* arose. *Assure* should be eliminated from insurance language since it adds nothing but confusion and misunderstanding.

The insurance industry could do worse than adapt to the use of the distinctive "ee" suffix, and thus describe the second party to the insurance contract as "insuree." The value of this suffix was illustrated by the Securities & Exchange Commission which, in an exhaustive opinion on the disseminating of so-called inside information (or tips) on publicly held stocks, found it necessary to use the terms *tipper* and *tippee* to describe provider and acceptor.

Underwriter

The word *underwriter* when used as a synonym for *insurer* is a grievous sin against good semantics, since it is also used, and correctly, to describe the employee within an insurance company whose duty it is "to select risks for insurance and to determine in what amounts and on what terms they will be accepted by the insurer."[2]

Life and Casualty

There are two broad divisions of insurance—life and casualty. This comes about because the states, which license insurers, divide the business in this manner.

The life insurance industry writes life insurance contracts and annuity contracts. These two lines of insurance are not permitted to the casualty insurers. Exclusive areas for casualty insurers are property and liability insurance, surety and fidelity coverages. Accidental death and dismemberment insurance and virtually all forms of health insurance such as hospital, surgical and other medical coverages can be written by both life insurers and casualty insurers.

---

[2] *Dictionary of Insurance Terms.* Dr. Ralph H. Blanchard, ed. Chamber of Commerce of the United States.

Self Insurance

Because this is a study of risk management, it is particularly important to examine the terminology used in describing the treatment of risk available to the party subject to the risk. If the party contracts to transfer the risk to another, the process is universally described as *insuring* the risk. *Self insurance* has been defined in the Dictionary of Insurance Terms as "setting aside of funds by an individual or organization to meet one's or its losses, and accumulation of a fund to absorb fluctuations in the amount of loss, the losses being charged against the funds so set aside or accumulated." *Self assumption* of a risk is something different. It is a process in which a person or organization consciously accepts the risks of loss without making provision for it either by insuring it or self insuring it.

A respectable group of insurance semanticists prefer to call this process *risk retention.* I believe the word *retention* is best used to describe funds paid to the insurer by the insured. *Gross retention* means funds not yet used for losses. *Net retention* means funds remaining after deducting losses and other expenses incurred for the insured. Despite what I believe or like, the term *self-insured retention* is increasingly being used to describe a program whereby a party susceptible to a risk consciously accepts that risk without insurance whether or not the risk is provided for by means of a self insurance reserve.

Fire Protection

People generally and risk managers in particular should know how fire protection engineers, the firms providing their equipment, and the manufacturers of building materials, describe the capability of those materials.

For years people in this specialty suffered because of the use of two key terms. One of these was the term *fireproof,* which is misleading. No material or building is fireproof. So the term *fire resistive* is being substituted to describe the condition of materials in buildings which the public generally would call fireproof.

A second key term was *inflammable,* which was ambivalent because of the prefix "in." Practitioners developed the term *non-flammable* to be used as the antonym of *flammable.*

To provide more detailed explanations of fire protection terms we are appending to this chapter an Explanation of Terms from the Fire Protection Handbook of the National Fire Protection Association.

EXPLANATION OF TERMS

The terms in this HANDBOOK are in accordance with general usage and dictionary definitions. Those listed below are used in this HANDBOOK with the meanings indicated. A number of special terms are individually defined in the text. See the Index for the location of these definitions.

Combustible is used to refer to a material or structure which can burn. *Combustible* is a relative term; many materials which will burn under one set of conditions will not burn under others, e.g., structural steel is noncombustible, but fine steel wool is combustible. The term *combustible* does not usually indicate ease of ignition, burning intensity, or rate of burning, except when modified by a word such as *highly*, as in *highly combustible interior finish.*

Fire prevention refers primarily to measures directed towards avoiding the inception of fire. *Fire prevention,* as used in the HANDBOOK, is not synonymous with *fire protection.*

Fireproof has been officially discontinued in NFPA publications as misleading, as no material is immune to the effects of fire of sufficient intensity and duration, although *fireproof* as popularly used is synonymous with *fire resistive* as defined here. *Fireproof* is also used in quotation marks in some references to popular misconceptions of the fire resistive properties of buildings.

Fire load refers to the amount of combustibles present in a given situation, usually expressed in terms of weight of combustible material per square foot. This measure is employed frequently to calculate the degree of fire resistance required to withstand a fire or to judge the rate of application and quantity of extinguishing agent needed to control or extinguish a fire.

Fire protection is used in two senses. The general sense, typified by the use of the term in the National Fire Protection Association name, includes everything relating to the prevention, detection, and extinguishment of fire; the reduction of losses and other matters covered in the HANDBOOK; as well as both the safeguarding of human life and the preservation of property. In its specific sense, *fire protection* refers to the methods of providing for fire control or fire extinguishment.

Fire resistance is a relative term, used with a numerical rating or modifying adjective to indicate the extent to which a material or structure resists the effect of fire, e.g., "*fire resistance* of 2 hours as measured on the Standard Time-Temperature Curve."

Fire resistive refers to properties or designs to resist the effects of any fire to which a material or structure may be expected to be subjected. *Fire resistive* materials or assemblies of materials are noncombustible, but noncombustible materials are not necessarily *fire resistive; fire resistive* implies a higher degree of fire resistance than noncombustible. *Fire-rèsistive* construction is defined in Section 6, Chapter 5 in terms of specified fire resistance as measured by the Standard Time-Temperature Curve.

Fire retardant, in general, denotes a substantially lower degree of fire resis-

Source: *The Fire Protection Handbook,* 14th Edition, page A-39.

tance than fire resistive and is often used to refer to materials or structures which are combustible in whole or in part, but have been subjected to treatments or have surface coverings to prevent or retard ignition or the spread of fire under the conditions for which they are designed.

Flameproof, flameproofing are misleading terms and their use is discouraged in favor of *flame retardant* or *flame resistant.*

Flame resistant is a term that may be used more or less interchangeably with *flame retardant* (see below).

Flame retardant refers to materials, usually decorative, which due to chemical treatment or inherent properties do not ignite readily or propagate flaming under small to moderate exposure. It is the preferable term to denote chemicals, processes, paints, or coatings used for the treatment of such materials as fabrics, foliage, Christmas trees and similar items in the class of decorations or furnishings. Flame retardant denotes a lower degree of resistance than fire retardant.

Flammable is used to describe a combustible material that ignites very easily, burns intensely, or has a rapid rate of flamespread. *Flammable* is used in a general sense without reference to specific limits of ignition temperature, rate of burning, or other property. Where exact differentiations are necessary, numerical divisions are made, such as Class I and Class II *flammable* liquids. *Flammable* and *inflammable* are identical in meaning. *Flammable* is used in preference to *inflammable* to avoid possible confusion due to the prefix *in-* which indicates the negative in many words, e.g., *incombustible.*

Flashover refers to the phenomenon of a slowly developing fire (or radiant heat source) producing radiant energy at wall and ceiling surfaces. The radiant feedback from those surfaces gradually heats the contents of the fire area, and when all the combustibles in the space have become heated to their ignition temperature, simultaneous ignition occurs as from a pilot ignition source.

Hazard (hazardous) is used in different senses. One is to indicate materials of more than average combustibility or materials that are dangerous because of their explosibility, instability, or toxicity, e.g., cellulose nitrate which is *hazardous* because of ease of ignition and intensity of burning, or a combustible dust which presents a *hazardous* condition when in suspension. A second use of *hazardous* is to describe the over-all degree of fire vulnerability of a property, thinking in terms of its fire load. For example, sprinklers require closer spacing in an extra *hazard* occupancy than in an ordinary *hazard* occupancy. A third use of *hazard* is to describe rate of burning, e.g., wood in the form of shavings is more *hazardous* than in the form of solid timber. Then, too, the term *hazard* is used to describe the nature of the fire problem, e.g., common *hazards* are ignition sources encountered in almost every class of property (smoking, heating, electrical, etc.) while special *hazards* are those considered peculiar to an individual property, e.g., dip tanks, spray booths, drying ovens in a metalworking plant. There is no sharp line of demarcation between common and special *hazards* as the same potential fire cause may be considered a common *hazard* in one occupancy and a special *hazard* in another.

Incombustible has the same meaning as *noncombustible,* but may be subject to misunderstanding due to the prefix *in-*.

Inflammable. See **Flammable.**

Noncombustible means *not combustible.*

Nonflammable means *not flammable.*

3

The Scope and Dynamics of Risk Management

Just what does a risk manager and the employees of a risk management department do? Do they spend their working days delineating the corporation's accidental risks from its business risks and then remonstrate with top management to abate the accidental risks forthwith? Probably not—or at least not for long.

Over the years the corporate risk management department has fallen heir to many clerical and administrative tasks that are as essential to the success of the corporation as those tasks assigned to any other department.

Although these tasks vary from one corporation to another, we present here a fairly representative list of responsibilities of a typical corporate risk management department.

Economical Protection

The risk manager and the department must make sure that the corporation receives the best and most economical protection from its insurance contracts. This is true whether the risk manager has complete and final binding authority or whether recommendations must be approved by higher management.

Insurance is complicated, its workings oblique, and its terminology obscure. So most corporations rely heavily on their risk management department to make sure the corporate purpose is well served, often without too much detailed supervision. Corporate insurance is not inexpensive and contracts often call for six-figure annual expenditures. Even seven-figure expenditures are becoming commonplace.

Once, when discussing an impending auto insurance price increase in a state in which that coverage is compulsory, an articulate political pundit expressed the opinion that, with the exception of income taxes, no expenditure was more resented by the voters than auto insurance. This is because, he said, it is intangible, its benefits are remote, and it has an inherent negative quality. The discerning corporate risk manager recognizes that insurance expenditures are unappreciated by top management for exactly the same reasons.

Loss Prevention

The many insurance contracts of corporations specify a multitude of things that are to be accomplished by both parties—the insurer and the insured. It is the risk management department's responsibility to see that these things are accomplished.

Over the years, certain equipment used by the corporation has been deemed hazardous enough by governmental authority to require periodic inspection of the equipment and other loss prevention activity. It has been customary for the insurer underwriting the risks to do this inspecting. Thus, the insurer for boiler and pressure vessel explosion invariably inspects those devices as required by state law or municipal ordinance. Similarly, the insurer for elevator liability performs the mandatory inspections of those devices. Most fire insurers, particularly where huge concentrated insurable values are involved, make inspections and perform other loss prevention services to reduce fire hazards. They make certain that sprinklers and other fire fighting apparatus are in working order.

All of this insurer inspection activity generates a sizeable amount of paperwork between the insurer and the corporation. The insurer's reports, often recommending engineering, structural or procedural changes, must be evaluated and coordinated within the corporation. These evaluations are almost never the sole responsibility of the risk manager. The coordination required within the corporation is usually the responsibility of the risk manager. It is generally the "user" or "owner" department of the equipment that must agree to and then accomplish these changes.

Accounting

The corporate insurance program requires specialized accounting. Whether or not the risk management department allocates the insurance costs throughout the "using" divisions and departments of the company, the risk manager must be familiar with the method used to allocate, because it takes specialized knowledge to make sure that this allocation is fair and equitable.

Underwriting

To reduce clerical work, corporations strive to provide the data that the insurer needs to underwrite the corporate risks in a systematic simple form, with enough detail that the premium is fair and adequate. Yet the procedure for accumulating the data should be as inexpensive as possible.

If you and I were to buy another car or add a room to our house, we would have to advise our insurer to give us protection for these new items. This is not an onerous task for us, because such events occur infrequently in our personal lives. A corporation, with insurable values in the hundreds of millions of dollars is constantly adding to and deleting from its plant and equipment. Similarly, a corporation with hundreds or thousands of vehicles is constantly adding to and deleting from its fleet. So the task of keeping the insurer informed is a complicated one.

Various ways are used to provide the insurer with data essential to underwriting. For underwriting property risks, a corporation may report the acquisition or disposal of "significant" values of buildings and equipment—say $250,000 or more, and then rely on taking an average of the total of the values at the beginning and end of the time period used. For inventory values, which can fluctuate widely, due to seasonal and other cycles, it is often deemed fair to both insurer and the insured that an average inventory complement be established upon which the insurance premium will be based. Thus, it is assumed that the times when the location will have inventory greater than the complement will be offset by the times when the actual inventory will be less than the complement. In the event of loss the insurer will pay the amount of the loss.

Business Interruption

Values for business interruption insurance are difficult to fix. This insurance coverage, designed to reimburse the corporation for the contribution to fixed costs and profit arising from the destroyed location, depends upon the exposure to loss, which in turn depends upon the level of plant production, the stability of the market for the product and other highly variable elements.

The risk management department must have a broad enough knowledge of all aspects of company operations to make sure that countless details are properly executed and the corporate interest is served. It is essential that the tasks described above are carried out successfully. Most of this administrative work deals with corporate risks which most people in the corporation are aware of and upon which the corporation has decided to insure or self insure or retain. It is more difficult to ascertain and evaluate the new risks to which the corporation is subject than to reevaluate those corporate risks which have changed in intensity and potentiality.

The Dynamics of Risk

The dynamics of risk is fascinating. It deals with the drives and outside influences which keep changing the risks in form and substance and in how these risks are regarded.

A wayward cousin of mine once felt that he knew how to earn his living by betting on horse races. His system was to double his bet after each loss until he obtained a winner. One does not have to be an expert in geometric progression to know that, after a very few losses and consequent doubling up, my cousin was making bets of considerable magnitude. It wasn't long before he was forced to abandon his system. I once asked him what was the largest bet he had made. His answer was, "My last two dollars!"

This illustrates one aspect of the dynamics of risk, which is that a loss can have a vastly different effect upon different corporations, or even upon the same corporation at different times. A corporation with hundreds of millions of dollars of retained earnings is not greatly affected by a large uninsured loss. But a corporation with little retained earnings would have to omit its dividend as a result of suffering the loss. It is apparent that the intensity of loss, measured by data within the corporation, is a factor in the dynamics of the risk.

Importance of Timing

Consider also the timing element. To illustrate, assume that a person requires major surgery that will cost $100,000. Most persons would find it extremely difficult, if not impossible, to get together this sum in the 90 to 120 days, in which the medical profession assumes such charges will be paid. On the other hand, if this cost could be paid over an extended period of years at the rate of $100 a month, most persons could absorb it without too much trouble.

A serious problem arises where a loss occurs and there is not enough time to take care of it. In such instances, relatively small amounts become very important. This is the rationale behind some seemingly inconsistent indemnification provisions in insurance contracts. A good example is the typical provision in some medical insurance contracts that provide for reimbursement of hospital expenses in full, while stipulating something less than full reimbursement for surgical and other medical costs. Hospital bills are generally expected to be paid weekly and, at the latest, at the time a patient is discharged. Many of us pay our doctors' bills on a much more leisurely schedule. This timing element is an important one to consider in any plan for reimbursement via an insurance contract. A contract that ignores such an element is said to be unresponsive to the need of the insured.

Risks Constantly Change

Risk, like life itself, is everywhere around us, and like life, it is constantly changing. Virtually every aspect of living is susceptible to risk and the chance of risk. If the owner of a year-round home buys a hunting lodge, the risk of loss of property is doubled. The exposure is doubled.

The acquisition of a second automobile by a family results in an obvious increase in risk. It is not so obvious that the risk of loss to the owner of a house inexorably increases as the value of the house increases due to inflation and other factors. It is just as probable that the risk of fortuitous loss will probably increase as the house gets older and more hazardous.

It is logical that all corporations of any size should have someone on the payroll responsible for the analysis and disposition of these fortuitous risks. Large corporations should have an entire department devoted to this activity.

4

The Law of Large Numbers

The law of large numbers is basic to risk management. Insurance companies couldn't get along without it, any more than mathematicians could get along without the multiplication table.

The law of large numbers sprang from the study of probability, which is a part of the science of logic. The concept is simple. When we say the law of averages is catching up with us, we really are referring to the law of large numbers. A discerning bishop, Joseph Butler (1692–1752), once said, "Probability is the very guide of life."

Poisson's Law

The law of large numbers was first propounded by Simeon Denis Poisson (1781–1840), a French mathematician and logician. He studied such human traits as drunkenness and absent mindedness, which might seem to occur at random. But he observed that these traits showed up at a predictable frequency—when large aggregates of individuals are included. That is the key—large numbers.

A vital example of this law is the incidence of early death. When we look only at small groups of people, such as single families or even an entire community, the death of a 25-year-old person appears to be an almost isolated event. Yet the actuarial tables tell us that out of every 100,000 persons 25 years old, 193 will die.

Within groups and for specific, short periods of time, there can be considerable deviation from the norm. But as the number of persons or events in the sample increases, the closer we come to the number predicted by Poisson's law of large numbers.

Other Pioneers

While there is general agreement among students of the subject that Poisson was the first to name the phenomenom being described as the law of large numbers, there is no agreement that he discovered the principle alone. Richard von Mises, in his work, "Probability, Statistics and Truth," expressed the opinion that Poisson's work is a generalization of a theorem formulated by Jacques Bernouilli (1654–1705). Thereafter, von Mises refers to the Bernouilli-Poisson theorem.[1]

John Maynard Keynes has said that Poisson's work on the law of great numbers, as the British prefer to call it, was but an extension of Bernouilli's theorem.[2]

Poisson's studies were further simplified by the Belgian statistician and astronomer, Adolphe Jacques Lambert Quetelet (1796–1874), who further inferred that Poisson's "law" was a consequence of the mathematical theory of probability. Quetelet was so impressed with the law that he advocated its use as a base for a system of social physics.

Probability as a Philosophical Concept

When we talk about probability, we should keep clearly in mind that this concept has both a philosophical sense and a mathematical aspect. Writing in the Encyclopedia Americana, Ernest Nagel, professor of philosophy at Columbia University (faculty emeritus), defines probability in its philosophical sense. He calls it "that branch of general logic which analyzes nondemonstrative inferences or arguments as distinguished from demonstrative ones."

Nagel adds that a nondemonstrative argument is one where a conclusion does not necessarily or with certainty stand proven as true by the arguments advanced in support of it. In contrast, a demonstrative argument is one in which the conclusion has to be true if the arguments advanced in support of it are true.

In any such analysis of nondemonstrative inferences, when we are presented with arguments supporting the truth of the conclusion, but if the arguments are not strong enough to render the conclusion certain, the next analytical step is to try to measure the degree of certainty involved. When we hear comments beginning with "the chances are . . ." or "the odds are . . ." this process of assigning weight to the arguments is going on. This assignment of weight is a constant process in the decision making of virtually all aspects of living. So it does support Bishop Butler's comment, mentioned earlier, that probability is the very guide of life.

---

[1] von Mises, Richard, *Probability, Statistics and Truth,* trans. Hilda Geiringer, New York, the Macmillan Company 1957, pp. 104–106.

[2] Keynes, John Maynard, *A Treatise on Probability,* New York and Evanston, Harper and Row, 1962, pp. 332–334.

The Mathematical Approach

The mathematical theory of probability is an extension of the philosophical process. In it we seek to assign numerical measurement to the abstract concept of likelihood. However, the mathematical theory of probability encompasses much more than merely a mathematical determination of the "chances of" or "odds on" a certain event occurring. This theory encompasses a whole branch of mathematical activity, including statistics, use of random variables, combinations and permutations that are part of the field of operations research, which uses specific and relative likelihood as a base.

The difference between the philosophical and the mathematical concept of probability is a subtle one. Corporate risk managers and those who seek to help them in their work must be aware of the distinction, since both concepts can be, and often have to be, brought into use in the successful disposition of risk management problems.

The fact that one cannot place a dollar value on the various possibilities which may occur does not mean that such possibilities can be ignored. The best service that corporate risk managers can give their corporations in this area of nonquantifiable risk is to isolate, identify and announce the existence of these risks. This accomplishes, first, the identification of potential loss, and permits taking steps to ameliorate or prevent the loss. Second, it eliminates unpleasant surprises which top management abhors.

Lessening the Risks

Having successfully isolated, identified and announced the existence of the fortuitous risk, what should risk managers do next? The obvious answer is that they must do whatever they can to lessen the risk. From the very nature of these risks, we know that no one can completely eliminate the possibility of loss. But, the law of large numbers can be used to ameliorate, or tame, the risks, although this is not an easy principle to apply.

Let's see what the experts have to say. von Mises states flatly, "to apply the theory of probability, we must have a practically unlimited sequence of uniform observations."[3] At the same time, he introduces a new term, "the collective." He defines it as a sequence of uniform processes. A collective, he adds, must exist be-

[3] von Mises, *Probability, Statistics and Truth,* ibid p. 11.

fore we can speak of probability. The definition of probability is only concerned with "the probability of encountering a certain attribute in a given collective."[4]

von Mises further states that the probability of winning a battle, as an example, has no place in the theory of probability, because we cannot think of a collective to which it belongs.[5] Other aspects of a collective, according to von Mises, are that the relative frequencies of the attributes must present limiting values and that these limiting values must remain the same in all partial sequences which may be selected from the original one in an arbitrary way.[6]

We learn from Keynes that, in the application of probability, the principle of indifference must exist. He says, "events are equally probable if we have not the slightest knowledge of the conditions under which each of them is going to occur."[7]

These observations about probability can best be illustrated by a simple example. Say you are tossing a coin and you have had a phenomenal streak of heads coming up—say 50 times in a row. Now you are about to toss the coin for the fifty-first time.

Most nonexperts of probability would assume that the chances of this toss coming up on the tails side would be immeasurably greater than on the heads side. The experts tell us "no." Despite the long streak of heads, the chances are still 50–50.

Stability of Statistical Frequencies

Finally, Keynes comes to a most important aspect of the concept of probability in general and the law of large numbers in particular. He says:

"The existence of numerous instances of the Law of Great Numbers, or of something of the kind, is absolutely essential for the importance of Statistical Induction." Apart from this, the more precise parts of statistics, the collection of facts, for the prediction of future frequencies and associations, would be nearly useless.

"But the 'Law of Great Numbers' is not at all a good name for the principle which underlies Statistical Induction. The 'Stability of Statistical Frequencies' would be a much better name for it."

---

[4] von Mises, *Probability, Statistics and Truth,* ibid p. 12.
[5] von Mises, *Probability, Statistics and Truth,* ibid p. 15.
[6] von Mises, *Probability, Statistics and Truth,* ibid p. 24.
[7] Keynes, *A Treatise on Probability,* ibid p. 75.

The former suggests, as perhaps Poisson intended to suggest, but which is certainly false, that every class of event shows statistical regularity of occurrence if only one takes a sufficient number of instances of it. It also encourages the method of procedure, by which it is thought legitimate to take any observed degree of frequency or association, which is shown in a fairly numerous set of statistics, and to assume with insufficient investigation that, because the statistics are numerous, the observed degree of frequency is therefore stable.

Observation shows that some statistical frequencies are, within narrower or wider limits, stable. But stable frequencies are not very common, and cannot be assumed lightly.

"The gradual discovery that there are certain classes of phenomena in which, though it is impossible to predict what will happen in each individual case, there is nevertheless a regularity of occurrence if the phenomena be considered together in successive sets, gives the clue to the abstract inquiry upon which we are about to embark."[8]

Where risk management is concerned, Keynes' observations sound a warning and a great opportunity.

The Role of Probability

Probability, in its mathematical sense, is used in the insuring process. Mortality tables are used in determining life insurance premium rates. As for property and liability coverages, the expected loss rates are developed from past loss data and are used to determine the premium to be charged to insure against future losses of that class.

To the loss data so developed, a credibility factor is applied. The application of this factor in itself recognizes an aspect of the law of large numbers. It says that the larger the sample, the more probable that the sample will conform to the norm.

The practical effect of applying credibility tables to loss data for rate making is to penalize the lesser amount of loss data so treated, at least when compared with the treatment accorded the larger amounts. Past loss data are extremely important in calculating the premium to be charged for insurance against risk. Insurers strive to distribute the losses of the few among the many who bear the risk of such losses.

---

[8] Keynes, *A Treatise on Probability,* ibid p. 336.

Finding the Premium

To illustrate, let's turn again to the risk of early death. According to the mortality tables widely used among life insurers, 251 out of every 100,000 persons will die at age thirty-five in any year. It follows, therefore, that a life insurance company would have to charge $2.51 per $1,000. of coverage to provide for the mortality risk of these thirty-five-year old persons. This illustrates the oft quoted precept that insurance is actually a pooling arrangement which assesses the many who are subject to the risk to pay for the losses of the few who actually suffer the losses.

A mortality table does more than describe the number who will die, actuarially speaking, in a given year. It also defines the insurable classes, since it establishes and defines the risk-sharing entities, thus permitting the life insurance industry to arrange a pooling of risk.

We say "actuarially speaking" because, even in a group large enough to achieve 100 percent credibility, there can be substantial deviation from the norm in the actual experience of any group. These deviations from the norm, plus the inherent difficulty in dealing in future events, is the reason why insurers place a loading for uncertainty (the insurers call it contingency) in their calculation of the price to be charged. Although this is probably necessary, it is an anomaly, since it protects the insurers against uncertainty, while they purport to be protecting their customers against uncertainty.

Measuring Inherent Probabilities

Calculating life insurance premiums with exactness is extremely difficult because wide variations from the norm are possible. Yet calculating life insurance premiums is simple compared with calculating premiums for property or liability insurance. No neat risk-sharing entities, such as found in a mortality table, are available to property and liability insurers.

Whether we realize it or not, every decision we ever make involves our use of an element of probability. We are probably going to be better off if we do the thing we're going to do rather than if we do the many other things we are capable of doing instead. This element of probability is present in our decision of where to live, where to work and how to spend our money. In each case, whether we consciously realize it, we rationalize, based on the probabilities. Although we rarely come right down to placing

MORTALITY TABLE

1971 INDIVIDUAL ANNUITY MORTALITY TABLE

Male Age	Number Living	Deaths Each Year	Deaths Per 1,000	Expectancy, Years	% Living to 65	Male Age	Number Living	Deaths Each Year	Deaths Per 1,000	Expectancy, Years	% Living to 65
5	10,000.00	4.56	.456	71.69	81.35	60	8,735.82	107.01	12.25	20.83	93.12
6	9,995.44	4.24	.424	70.73	81.39	61	8,628.82	113.32	13.13	20.08	94.28
7	9,991.20	4.03	.403	69.75	81.42	62	8,515.50	119.84	14.07	19.34	95.53
8	9,987.18	3.92	.392	68.78	81.46	63	8,395.66	126.63	15.08	18.61	96.90
9	9,983.26	3.88	.389	67.81	81.49	64	8,269.03	133.83	16.19	17.89	93.38
10	9,979.38	3.89	.390	66.84	81.52	65	8,135.19	141.59	17.41	17.17	100.00
11	9,975.49	3.96	.397	65.86	81.55	66	7,993.60	150.02	18.77	16.47	....
12	9,971.52	4.04	.405	64.89	81.58	67	7,843.58	159.15	20.29	15.77	....
13	9,967.49	4.12	.413	63.91	81.62	68	7,684.44	169.00	21.99	15.09	....
14	9,963.37	4.20	.422	62.94	81.65	69	7,515.44	179.54	23.89	14.42	....
15	9,959.17	4.31	.433	61.97	81.69	70	7,335.90	190.73	26.00	13.76	....
16	9,954.85	4.42	.444	60.99	81.72	71	7,145.16	202.50	28.34	13.11	....
17	9,950.43	4.55	.457	60.02	81.76	72	7,942.66	214.76	30.93	12.48	....
18	9,945.89	4.68	.471	59.05	81.79	73	6,727.91	227.41	33.80	11.86	....
19	9,941.20	4.83	.486	58.07	81.83	74	6,500.50	240.36	36.97	11.26	....
20	9,936.37	5.00	.503	57.10	81.87	75	6,260.13	253.50	40.49	10.67	....
21	9,931.37	5.18	.522	56.13	81.91	76	6,006.64	266.65	44.39	10.10	....
22	9,926.19	5.40	.544	55.16	81.96	77	5,739.98	279.62	48.72	9.55	....
23	9,920.79	5.62	.566	54.19	82.00	78	5,460.36	292.13	53.50	9.01	....
24	9,915.17	5.86	.591	53.22	82.05	79	5,168.23	303.82	58.79	8.50	....
25	9,909.31	6.13	.619	52.25	82.10	80	4,864.41	314.26	64.60	7.99	....
26	9,903.18	6.44	.650	51.28	82.15	81	4,550.17	322.62	70.90	7.51	....
27	9,896.74	6.77	.684	50.32	82.20	82	4,227.55	328.35	77.67	7.05	....
28	9,889.97	7.14	.722	49.35	82.26	83	3,899.21	331.20	84.94	6.60	....
29	9,882.83	7.54	.763	48.39	82.32	84	3,568.01	331.37	92.87	6.16	....
30	9,875.29	7.99	.809	47.42	82.38	85	3,236.63	329.13	101.69	5.74	....
31	9,867.30	8.49	.860	46.46	82.45	86	2,907.50	324.63	111.65	5.34	....
32	9,858.82	9.03	.916	45.50	82.52	87	2,582.87	317.82	123.05	4.95	....
33	9,849.79	9.63	.978	44.54	82.59	88	2,265.06	308.33	136.12	4.57	....
34	9,840.15	10.29	1.046	43.58	82.67	89	1,956.73	295.60	151.07	4.21	....
35	9,829.86	11.03	1.122	42.63	82.76	90	1,661.13	279.14	168.04	3.87	....
36	9,818.83	11.82	1.204	41.68	82.85	91	1,381.99	258.64	187.15	3.55	....
37	9,807.01	12.70	1.295	40.73	82.95	92	1,123.36	234.17	208.46	3.26	....
38	9,794.31	13.68	1.397	39.78	83.06	93	889.18	206.19	231.89	2.98	....
39	9,780.63	14.76	1.509	38.83	83.18	94	683.00	175.63	257.15	2.73	....
40	9,765.87	15.95	1.633	37.89	83.30	95	507.37	144.01	283.84	2.50	....
41	9,749.92	17.44	1.789	36.95	83.44	96	363.35	113.21	311.57	2.30	....
42	9,732.48	19.47	2.000	36.02	83.59	97	250.15	85.10	340.21	2.11	....
43	9,713.01	21.95	2.260	35.09	83.76	98	165.04	61.03	369.77	1.94	....
44	9,691.06	24.90	2.569	34.17	83.95	99	104.02	41.63	400.19	1.79	....
45	9,666.16	28.24	2.922	33.25	84.16	100	62.39	26.92	431.41	1.65	....
46	9,637.92	31.98	3.318	32.35	84.41	101	35.47	16.44	463.31	1.53	....
47	9,605.94	36.06	3.754	31.46	84.69	102	19.04	9.44	495.76	1.41	....
48	9,569.88	40.46	4.228	30.57	85.01	103	9.60	5.07	528.60	1.31	....
49	9,529.42	45.17	4.740	29.70	85.37	104	4.53	2.54	561.69	1.21	....
50	9,484.25	50.12	5.285	28.84	85.78	105	1.98	1.18	594.88	1.13	....
51	9,434.13	55.28	5.860	27.99	86.23	106	0.80	0.50	628.02	1.05	....
52	9,378.84	60.60	6.461	27.15	86.74	107	0.30	0.19	660.95	.98	....
53	9,318.24	66.05	7.088	26.33	87.30	108	0.10	0.07	693.50	.92	....
54	9,252.20	71.61	7.740	25.51	87.93	109	0.03	0.02	725.52	.86	....
55	9,180.58	77.27	8.417	24.71	88.61						
56	9,103.31	83.01	9.119	23.91	89.37						
57	9,020.30	88.85	9.850	23.13	90.19						
58	8,931.45	94.79	10.613	22.35	91.08						
59	8,836.66	100.84	11.411	21.59	92.06						

1981 BEST'S FLITCRAFT COMPEND

numbers or ratios or fractions in analyzing our desires, we still are really applying the mathematical theory of probability to decide our course of action.

It is no exaggeration to say that corporate risk management is devoted exclusively to consciously measuring inherent probabilities. For the risk manager, the "event" is the potential loss to the corporation. How does one quantify loss probabilities? The relative quality called for in the definition requires that the event—the loss when it occurs—be compared with some sort of base. von Mises calls this base, "collective."[9] Of necessity, the probabilities must be expressed as fractions, with the probability of occurring as the numerator, and the base as the denominator.

How Mortality Tables Work

A good way to study this subject in more detail is to examine once more the most widely used probability table in existence—the mortality table. All of us know that, despite the neat calculations and orderly rows of numbers, the occurrence of death among the population does not take place with the regularity that such orderliness suggests. These tables are approximations of what does happen. Note that, although a whole year is added in the age column, less than a year is always deducted in the life expectancy column.

Shifting Conditions

Doughty risk takers in property insurance attempt to classify the structures they insure by type of construction. They emphasize the degree of resistance to loss, such as combustibility, what the structures are to be used for, the relative availability of fire fighting capability, and the presence of fire prevention or extinguishing equipment within the structure.

All of these features can change with the passage of time. Then there are the variations found outside the structure, such as inflation and changing patterns of the neighborhood where the structure is located. These can greatly change the degree of risk. And they present to the insurer the herculean task of establishing the proper risk-sharing fee—the premium—that should be charged to cover the losses that could ensue.

---

[9] von Mises, *Probability, Statistics and Truth,* ibid p. 12.

5

Loss Measurement And Control

The corporate risk manager, whether or not directly responsible for the corporation's safety and loss prevention functions, should take an interest in corporate loss control.

The key index for analyzing and measuring industrial accidents is the Z16.1 index published by the American National Standards Institute. It is called "Method of Recording and Measuring Work Injury Experience." By this index, industrial accidents of a chargeable nature are measured by both frequency and severity.

On the frequency scale each accident of a chargeable nature has a value of one, regardless of how severe it might be. According to the plan, a chargeable accident is one severe enough that medical attention is required and the employee is unable to report for work the day following the accident. For every day that the injured employee is unable to work, this accident develops a charge of one person day.

A typical report of person days lost from injuries is given in Table I. This table also shows, at the right, the number of person days representing vehicle accidents which could have been prevented if good safety practices were adhered to.

TABLE I
Safety Department Second Quarter Safety Report

Injuries and Rates Again Improve

There were 131 fewer disabling injuries reported for the 12 months ending 6/30/79 than during the same period a year ago. All but two of the major divisions shared in this decrease. The corporation rate dropped correspondingly to 13.6 lost-time injuries per million person hours worked from 14.9 a year ago.

Four major divisions have so far attained 12 months-to-date rates close to or better than their 1978 disabling injury goals.

Like Quarterly Rates Compared

A comparison of the same quarterly periods a year apart has been introduced in this report to further assist in interpreting accident and injury rate trends.

DIVISION	DISABLING INJURY RATES					PREVENTABLE VEHICLE ACCIDENT RATES				
	2nd Quarter		12-Months Ending		GOALS	2nd Quarter		12-Months Ending		GOALS
	1979	1978	6/30/79	6/30/78	This Yr	1979	1978	6/30/79	6/30/78	This Yr
1	19.7	23.3	27.9	20.9	20.5	4.1	7.2	5.4	7.2	4.0
2	7.5	9.1	8.4	6.6	8.0	0.0	0.7	1.2	2.2	2.5
3	6.4	7.4	8.5	10.5	3.5	2.4	6.5	5.9	8.2	3.6
4	27.4	10.2	23.2	27.7	28.9	0.0	12.7	5.5	14.2	6.0
5	0.0	6.2	1.5	7.4	5.0	0.0	0.0	13.9	21.4	7.1
6	15.6	21.4	18.7	19.3	13.4	7.7	12.9	10.8	14.0	9.4
7	31.3	32.8	32.9	14.3	20.0	10.5	20.6	11.4	14.0	11.0
8	37.6	38.4	47.4	38.4	30.1	7.1	18.6	19.0	25.3	14.4
9	8.9	29.7	17.3	21.8	11.5	3.2	7.2	6.1	7.2	5.5
10	7.4	13.9	10.2	15.6	9.3	9.8	11.9	11.7	13.0	9.2
11	20.4	25.7	21.6	25.3	16.1	11.2	20.5	13.4	19.4	13.3
12	16.5	15.1	18.9	19.5	15.9	6.2	7.9	10.4	9.8	7.1
13	7.2	7.1	6.0	6.1	4.8	6.1	5.1	5.9	9.0	6.0
14	12.5	9.2	8.4	25.6	9.7	0.0	0.0	9.4	16.3	8.7
15	11.3	13.1	13.6	14.9	9.3	4.1	8.6	7.3	10.1	6.9

If the system measured frequency only, a minor accident, such as a cut on the hand would have the same value as a major accident involving the loss of an arm or leg. So the severity index of Z16.1 was devised to distinguish between minor and major accidents. The basic unit in this severity index is still the lost person day described above. However, with serious accidents involving the loss of major members of the body, a series of charges are made based upon the period. Thus the death of an employee is quantified as 6000 person days lost. The loss of an arm or a leg is quantified at 4500 days. This attempts to give perspective to the frequency index. Other time charges in days are given in Table II.

TABLE II
American Standard Z16.1
Table of Scheduled Time Charges (Days)

A. For Loss of Member—Traumatic or Surgical

Fingers, Thumb, and Hand

Amputation involving all or part of bone	Thumb	Fingers: Index	Middle	Ring	Little
Distal Phalange	300	100	75	60	50
Middle Phalange	—	200	150	120	100
Proximal Phalange	600	400	300	240	200
Metacarpal	900	600	500	450	400
Hand at Wrist—3000					

Toe, Foot and Ankle

Amputation involving all or part of bone	Great Toe	Each of Other Toes
Distal Phalange	150	35
Middle Phalange	—	75
Proximal Phalange	300	150
Metatarsal	600	350
Foot at Ankle—2400		

Arm

Any point above elbow, including shoulder joint	4500
Any point above wrist and at or below elbow	3600

Leg

Any point above knee	4500
Any point above ankle and at or below knee	3000

B. Impairment of Function

One Eye (loss of sight), whether or not there is sight in the other eye	1800
Both Eyes (loss of sight), in one accident	6000
One Ear (complete indust. loss of hearing), whether or not there is hearing in the other ear	600
Both Ears (complete indust. loss of hearing), in one accident	3000
Unrepaired Hernia	50

Chart of Scheduled Charges for Hand and Foot

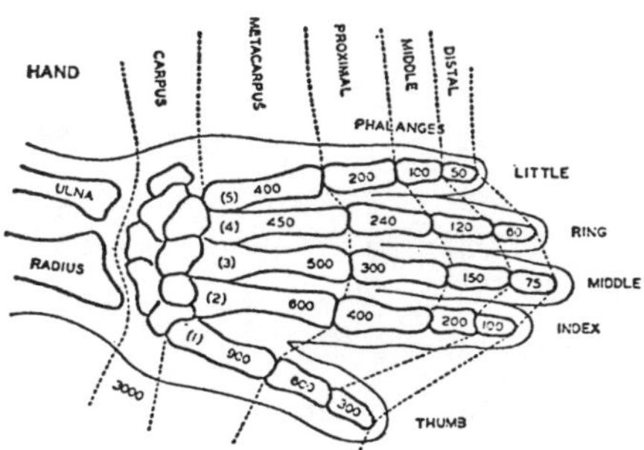

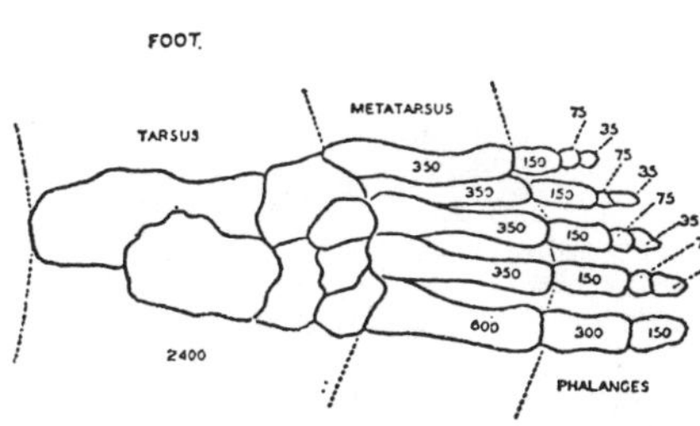

A typical corporate report of frequency and severity for a given period of time would look something like Table III.

A bar chart illustrating the typical trend of frequency rate and severity rate in a company over a period of years is shown in Table IV.

Critics Suggest Dollar Method

There are critics of this reporting method, despite the fact that it is widely used and is the standard approach among corporate safety and loss prevention personnel. The most frequent criticism is that the approach requires top management to learn a whole new set of standards, a new method of quantification, to see how the corporate safety program is doing.

TABLE III
Injury Experience—

	Labor Hours Worked	Disabling Injuries
GROUP I		
Division 1	23,303,139	55
Division 2	7,717,244	22[2]
Division 3	10,629,933	15
Division 4	755,577	4
TOTAL—Group I	42,405,893	96[2]
GROUP II		
Division 5	9,390,385	15
Division 6[1]	2,990,845	3
Division 7	17,467,881	33
Division 8	10,656,534	37[1]
Division 9	5,619,238	31[3]
TOTAL—Group II	46,124,883	119[4]
GROUP III		
Division 10	9,241,857	11
Division 11	3,521,916	8
Division 12	2,682,089	12
TOTAL—Group III	15,445,862	31
Division 13	24,668,032	25
Division		
Division 14[2]	494,102	1
Canada Limited	9,786,362	90
Consolidated Locations	8,482,626	10
Operating	147,407,760	379[6]
Sales	4,357,771	5
TOTAL OPERATING & SALES	151,765,531	384[6]

Fatalities are indicated by superscripts

[1] Division 6 started 6/1/78

The critics suggest using the dollar as a measure, since it is the measurement used in virtually all other departments of the corporation to measure performance. The rationale behind this is hard to refute. Virtually all industrial accidents result in some cost to the corporation. To quantify accidents in terms of dollar costs to the corporation does not need to be construed as callous disregard for the human suffering of employees and their families.

One insurer who specializes in workers' compensation analyzed several years of cost data to arrive at averages for the various accidents which occurred among the corporations that it insured. Table V shows typical cost elements which this insurer has indicated would be representative of the cost for several years. To my mind this type of presentation deserves wider acceptance among corporations than it appears to have received.

Table III—cont'd.

D.I. Frequency Rate			Severity Rate	
1979	1978	Days Charged	1979	1978
2.36	2.17	15,439	663	861
2.85	1.41	12,778	1,655	115
1.41	1.22	2,966	279	716
5.29	2.83	71	94	89
2.26	1.84	31,254	737	707
1.60	2.26	1,828	195	1,017
1.00	—	14	5	—
1.89	2.06	1,234	71	755
3.47	3.66	16,370	1,536	2,266
5.52	3.57	18,982	3,378	197
2.58	2.75	38,428	833	1,177
1.19	1.64	370	40	179
2.27	1.75	369	105	57
4.47	8.22	4,723	1,761	1,871
2.01	2.93	5,462	354	473
1.01	1.35	3,166	128	339
2.02	—	7	14	—
9.20	6.65	3,824	391	899
1.18	0.76	112	13	11
2.57	2.40	82,329	559	743
1.15	2.02	69	16	30
2.53	2.39	82,398	543	724

[2] Separate the experience for Division 14 not recorded prior to 1976.

TABLE IV

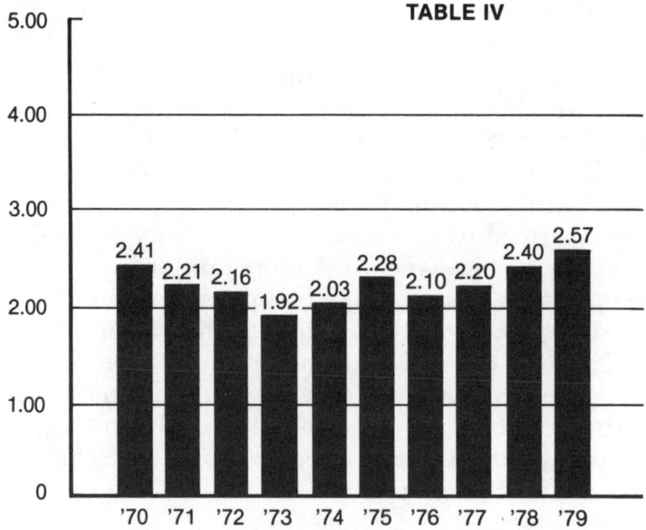

DISABLING INJURY FREQUENCY RATE
Number of disabling injuries per million employee hours worked.

Frequency rate for 1979

$\frac{379}{14.7} = 2.57$

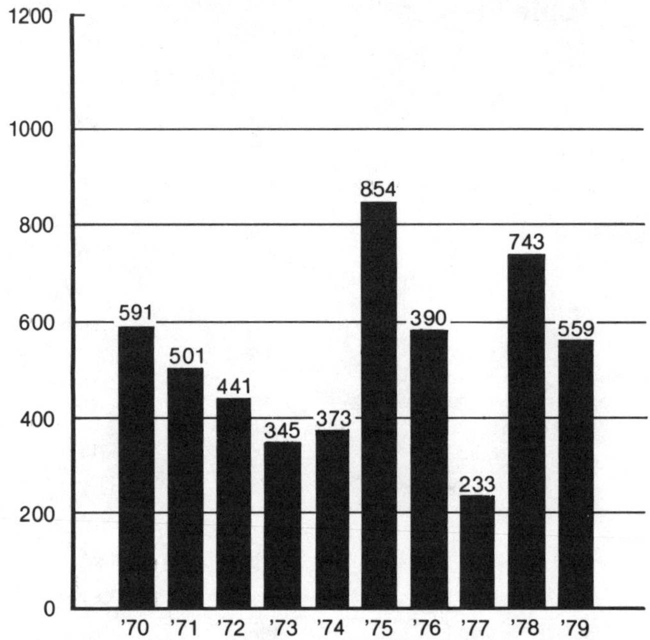

SEVERITY RATE
Number of days charge per million employee hours worked.

Severity rate for 1979

$\frac{82{,}329}{147.4} = 559$

Parts-of-Body Method

Another method often used to categorize industrial accidents is to indicate the part of the employee's body affected by the accident. The benefit of this method is that it often indicates possible steps to take to prevent further accidents. If eye accidents predomi-

TABLE V

Schedule of Charges

(Based on the injury cost analysis previously described)

Injury Involving Medical Cost only	$40
Fatality	$25,000
Permanent Total Disability	$5,000
Temporary Disability Involving No Permanent Results:	
For combined compensation and medical costs based on the number of working days during healing period estimated by doctor	$75 per day
Permanent Partial Disability:	
For combined compensation and medical costs based on the number of working days during healing period estimated by doctor	$75 per day
For the permanent disability based on doctor's estimate and the schedule to time charges from the American Standard Z16.1	$250 per day

nate among a group of employees, safety glasses and other equipment to protect the eyes probably should be made available. If the accidents include many involving injury to the employees' feet, safety shoes may be the answer.

One meaningful statistic was developed some 40 years ago by H. W. Heinrich. It is the ratio of known, direct dollar losses from industrial accidents to dollar losses which are indirect and largely nonquantifiable. In the original publication of this study, Mr. Heinrich suggested that a four-to-one ratio was appropriate. That is, for every dollar of known loss (medical expenses, indemnity to the injured employee, etc.) there were four additional dollars of indirect expenses which the corporation also sustained because of the accident. These indirect expenses could be the overtime premium paid to other employees to take care of the work of the injured employee, lost production, lost sales and similar indirect items.

Since this index was originally published, the data on which it was based have been systematically reviewed and the results published. The four-to-one ratio still appears to be a proper one.

Considering Equipment Needs

When it comes to property conservation, the corporate risk management department must be concerned with the optimum amount of loss protection equipment to be installed in the corporation's plants, warehouses and other facilities. This includes methods of installing sprinklers, the requisite number of fire walls in large facilities, use of explosion-proof roofs and a myriad of other technical details.

Enter OSHA

The passage of the Occupational Safety and Health Act (OSHA) in 1970 by the federal government brought a profound change in corporate loss control.

Briefly, if anyone can be brief about OSHA, the law was enacted to:

- Encourage employers and employees to reduce workplace hazards and to implement new or improved safety and health programs.
- Provide for research in occupational safety and health and develop innovative ways to deal with occupational safety and health problems.
- Establish "separate but dependent responsibilities and rights" for employers and employees to achieve better safety and health conditions.
- Maintain a reporting and recordkeeping system to monitor job-related injuries and illnesses.
- Establish training programs to increase the number and competence of occupational safety and health personnel.
- Develop mandatory job safety and health standards and enforce them effectively.
- Provide for the development, analysis, evaluation and approval of state occupational safety and health programs.

Following enactment came ten years of setting standards, governmental inspections and assorted controversies between and among employers, labor unions and the federal government.

Senator Richard Schweiker, who voted for OSHA in 1970, said in 1979 that he intended to introduce legislation reforming the act. He said he believed the 1970 act erred fundamentally by casting the government as a policeman "in a system of crime and punishment for more than four million workplaces in the United States" rather than directing the government's efforts to the five to ten percent of the workplaces where it is really needed. In 1981 Mr. Schweiker became Secretary of Health and Human Services in the Reagan Administration.

Whatever path OSHA takes, added emphasis will continue to be placed on loss control and job safety as far ahead as we can see.

6

Top Management's Role

To be effective, the corporate risk management department must achieve rapport and a satisfactory degree of coordination with all other departments and divisions of the corporation. This is not always easy to achieve. First we must understand where risk management is placed in the corporate organization and how the function is viewed by top management.

About 10 of every 20 risk managers report to the corporate treasurer, four to the financial vice president, one to the comptroller and one to the corporate counsel. The remaining four report to various other corporate officials, such as corporate secretary, production or quality control officials and/or the executive vice president. Only rarely does the risk manager report to the president or chief executive officer. This diversity of reporting by risk managers probably reflects their wide range of responsibilities—encompassing accounting, finance, law and operations.

The Organization Chart

If we look at the organization of a "typical," large corporation, we find five senior executives who report directly to the chief executive. They are responsible for finance, legal, corporate secretary, sales and operations (manufacturing, processing, etc.). There are other departments which often report directly to the chief executive, such as public relations, personnel, government relations, long range planning and research.

Let us assume there are five such department directors in addition to the five senior executives, making a total of ten reporting directly to the chief executive. These ten executives, with the chief executive, make up the top level of management.

The risk manager is almost never part of this top management group. In smaller companies risk managers are generally included in the second level of management, reporting to the financial vice president. In larger companies they are usually in the third level of management, reporting to the treasurer, who reports to the financial vice president.

One-Thirtieth of Top Management's Attention

The typical corporate organization chart has about 30 specialties having the same prominence as risk management. We can infer from this that risk management, on the average, commands about one-thirtieth of top management's time and attention. There are exceptions. In some companies—the airlines being a notable example—there are times when insurance costs are high and profits are low, giving rise to the anomaly of insurance costs equaling or exceeding the net profit of the company. In such cases corporate insurance costs and other aspects of risk management are sure to get most exacting attention from the top management of the company.

Affirmative vs. Defensive Specialties

The thirty or so specialties found in typical corporations could be divided into two categories—affirmative and defensive. The affirmative ones are those which make good things happen—which further the main objective of the company. Manufacturing, sales, advertising, sales promotion and new product development are affirmative in character. Internal auditing, security, quality control and risk management are defensive in character. These defensive specialities are devoted to keeping bad things from happening.

Top management is usually more comfortable dealing with the affirmative aspects than with the defensive ones. This is understandable because most people like to think positively. Moreover, those engaged in the positive aspects of corporate activity have the big advantage of being able to demonstrate their progress and their improvements in an affirmative way. Increase in sales or production is the most tangible evidence of improvement. Persons engaged in the defensive aspects of corporate activity have to be satisfied to demonstrate their success by showing a reduction in the undesirable.

It is probable that candidates for top management posts are selected from the affirmative areas of the corporation more often than from the defensive, so it is natural that prior training and experience make the people in affirmative jobs more comfortable in dealing with problems in these affirmative areas than in the defensive areas with which they have had less experience.

Members of top management are generalists; risk managers and other defensive practitioners are specialists.

The Most Defensive—Risk Management

Those who work in the defensive specialties in the corporate environment must allow for this inclination of top management in planning and in pursuing their objectives. Risk management, the most defensive of the defensive specialties, has problems all its own. For one, a major part of the risk manager's concern is for human injury, carrying with it the implication of human suffering. Most people, including members of top management, have difficulty concentrating for long on this negative aspect of human experience. Risk managers should be aware of this human tendency.

As we have observed, risk management evolved from the narrower concept of corporate insurance management, first in response to a need to guard against fortuitous risks by means other than buying insurance. It was logical that the insurance manager, already equipped to handle fortuitous risks, should be given the broader responsibilities of the risk manager.

The only problem was that top management was not ready to accept the concept of risk management. When faced with brand new fortuitous risks that cannot be passed on to an insurance company, a top manager rarely calls in the risk manager to discuss the best approach to further identify, evaluate, stabilize and fund it. By and large, corporate top management generally regards as the purview of the risk manager those risks which can be insured or taken care of by some substitute for insurance, such as self insurance.

This limited concept of top management is not likely to change quickly unless one of two things happens:

One would be that the corporation would begin, on a systematic basis, to pay for a whole host of fortuitous risks to which it is subject, by charging some percentage of the corporate profits as an expense and using it to build a reserve. Losses from these risks would then be charged against the reserve. At the present time such reserving is done only for risks of an insurable nature.

A second possibility, which would enlarge the risk manager's responsibility, is that the conventional insurance industry would agree to insure a whole gamut of a corporation's fortuitous risks.

Three Chances in 10,000

One of our truly intellectual risk managers gives a good description of an essential service the corporate risk manager must perform for a company's plant management. The manager begins with the expected loss rate typical of large, modern plants. This is probably about three cents per $100 of insurable value on a plant with a good sprinkler system and similar loss protection equipment.

If one accepts this ratio as reflecting the odds of the plant being destroyed by fire, we are talking about three out of 10,000 chances. My intellectual colleague asks, "How much time can the plant manager devote to the solution of a problem so unlikely to occur?" If the plant manager devoted any substantial amount of time to every risk which has three chances out of 10,000 of occurring, then there would be no time at all to devote to the main job of getting out the production and managing the employees.

Yet fire losses and their prevention are an important aspect of the successful operation of any corporation. The corporate risk manager and staff can successfully synthesize this in-plant risk into a corporatewide activity. This synthesis of risk should apply to all fortuitous risks in all plants of the corporation.

Is there a particular area of activity where risk management can be of more significant service to top management and hence to the company as a whole? It should be noted that in recent years the fortuitous risks which top management faces have increased substantially. These are risks which the corporate risk manager has not been able to help solve. Here is an illustration of this.

Insuring for Loss of Shelf Space

As perceptive a chief executive as I've ever known asked: "Why should a large company making products to retail primarily through supermarkets (where the battle for shelf space is intense) insure its manufacturing plant for $5 million for physical damage and $7 million for business interruption, but neglect to insure against the loss of shelf space, worth perhaps tens of millions, if the plant were out of production for a year or more?

Good risk management, of course, interests itself in the analysis of alternate and sole source of product facilities, and the potentialities of loss arising from it. We must wonder why the conventional insurance industry did not see fit to extend its risk-bearing facilities to the huge potential of this loss of shelf space. It appears that the new product departments of the insurance companies have not kept pace with the truly herculean risks which are being faced by customers for insurance.

Top management understands very well why business risks, being so much within the control of the risk taker, should not be eligible for the insuring process. But executives tend to regard all nonbusiness risks as a group and ask why all of them are not insurable.

Challenging the Risk Manager

The risk manager of one huge corporation reports on a discussion about the renewal of the corporation's business interruption insurance contract with the financial vice president:

The vice president said, "Tell me again what this coverage is designed to do." The risk manager explained that, if one of the company's plants were severely damaged or destroyed by fire or by one of the perils recited in the fire insurance contract's extended endorsement, the insurer would reimburse the corporation for the plant's fixed charges, the pay of the plant's permanent personnel and the profit lost by the plant's disablement or destruction during the time it took to rehabilitate the plant.

The vice president then asked, "How much of a loss are we talking about?" After a quick mental review of the probable maximum loss, the risk manager answered, "Probably in the neighborhood of $5 million."

The Greater Risk—Strikes

The vice president then asked, "You know that our Canadian operations are on strike and have been for some time now. If this continues for as long as we fear it will, no doubt the shutdown will cost the company much more than $5 million. Why should we insure against the remote risk of fire when we must take the much larger loss by strike without insurance?"

The risk manager started to explain in the manner of all risk managers, that insurance against strike loss is virtually impossible to obtain.

But this wasn't what the vice president had in mind. The thought wasn't that strike losses should be pooled with those of other companies through the insuring process. It was, why should the corporation make special provision to take care of a relatively small loss much less apt to occur when it can and must accept the consequences of the larger loss which will occur more often.

The risk manager asked, "Wouldn't the investment community, emphasizing as it does continuity in profit margins, react unfavorably to a $5 million loss which could have been insured and wasn't, while it would be understanding about a larger strike loss, since it is not insurable?"

The vice president was not persuaded and said: "Both the $10 million strike loss and the $5 million fire loss would be treated as a special, extraordinary charge in our financial reporting. Neither could even remotely affect our dividend payment. The investment community tends to take all truly extraordinary charges in stride, even those of a substantial amount. I see no reason why the investment community would react unfavorably to a special charge, especially if the overall effect was that the company saved money in the process." The final observation assumes that the corporation ultimately bears its own losses.

This corporate vice president is not an exception. This type of thinking increases with the increasing number and severity of truly uncontrollable risks. It presents a challenging problem to those of us who espouse the risk pooling concept.

7
Handling Risks Internally

Typically, risk managers are advisors rather than participants in the major operations of the corporations they serve. They have no line authority in such operations as production, sales and distribution. Instead they advise the heads of the departments and divisions.

This is as it should be. In fact, there is no other practical approach, because the possibility of loss runs through virtually every process and operation of the company. The only alternative would be to give risk managers authority coextensive with their chief executives.

Performing a staff function, risk managers are responsible in varying degrees along with the heads of the major departments they advise on risk control.

Corporate "Risk Handlers"

However, we should note that there are other "risk handlers" in the corporation, with varying degrees of responsibility to abate or eliminate some of the risks of loss in corporations.

For instance, corporations are subject to loss from employee dishonesty. When such losses occur, they can be recovered under the corporate insurance program through a fidelity bond or a "comprehensive 3 D" insurance contract (Dishonesty, Destruction, Disappearance).

The risk manager's responsibility for preventing the loss must be reconciled with the staff responsibility of the company audit department to prevent employee defalcations.

In a similar manner, product liability claims are invariably insured under the corporation's general liability insurance contract. We might generalize that, if valid products liability claims exist against the corporation to any substantial degree, they strongly suggest that quality control needs to be strengthened. Yet the quality control department is itself as much of a "risk handler" as is the risk management department.

The compliance department, a new entity on the corporate scene, is charged with seeing that employees comply with government and the corporation's own regulations and procedures. In so doing, it is dealing in the control and abatement of corporate risks of a highly specialized nature fully as much as is the corporate risk management department. In the absence of a compliance department, the corporation would probably rely on its legal department to perform this compliance function.

Risks Beyond Control

In some corporations one of the most sophisticated forms of risk analysis and abatement is performed with no reference to the risk management department at all. It is the use of commodity and currency trading to insure that the corporation does not suffer loss due to fluctuations in the prices of commodities and the rates of currency exchange. The simplicity and efficiency of this risk handling device should make most risk managers envious, struggling as they do with their mixed bag of hazards to be provided for.

A simple example will show how this procedure operates. An operator of an edible oil refinery contracts to sell the soybean oil output from the refinery for 18 cents a pound for the next several months. This means that soybeans must be obtained at about $12.00 per bushel. The operator buys contracts for future delivery on the Chicago Board of Trade. During the time the soybean oil is being refined, the price of beans increases to $14.00 per bushel. Our operator has guarded against this price rise, since the other party to the future transaction, invariably a speculator, must deliver beans at the $12.00 contract price.

In this example, the speculator has absorbed the risk and has lost money on the transaction. If the beans had gone down in price, the speculator would have made a profit on the contract. The refinery operator is not much concerned which way the price of beans goes. For a small fee—the price of the futures contract—the operator bought protection against loss fully as effectively as if it were a contract of insurance written by an insurance company.

Currency Fluctuations

Similarly, treasurers of large multinational corporations face the risk of loss from currency fluctuations and often gain protection by buying or selling the particular currency in question on the futures market. This form of risk handling is also outside the scope of the corporate risk management department.

Some companies with a great deal of other people's property in their possession, such as railroads, airlines, trucking companies, warehouses and hotels, have set up elaborate security departments to handle pilferage and other thefts. Large banks and department stores have done the same thing.

The work of these security departments is generally independent of the risk management department. If the loss is insured, however, as it invariably is, the corporation's risk management department will be responsible for processing the claim through to a conclusion with the insurer.

Charting the Three Party Relationship

The Risk Responsibility Chart depicts this three party relationship. It assumes that the function generally called corporate safety or loss prevention is part of the risk management department.

RISK RESPONSIBILITY CHART

	Responsibility of		
	Risk Management Department	**Operating Department (Production, (Sales Etc.)**	**Other "Risk Handling" Department**
Fire, windstorm and other extended coverage perils.	Yes	Yes	No
Other physical perils: flood, explosion, earthquake, etc.	Yes	Yes	No
Employee theft	Yes	Yes	Yes
Robbery, burglary, and other dishonesty insurable under a corporate 3 D policy.	Yes	Yes	Yes
Product defects (no products liability cases).	No	Yes	Yes
Product defects (with product liability cases involved).	Yes	Yes	Yes
Auto liability cases.	Yes	Yes	No
Other claims arising from bodily injury, property damage.	Yes	Yes	No

No department or person within a company is entitled to participate in the solution of a problem unless such participation aids in the solution. Under what conditions, then, should the risk management department be asked to contribute to a solution, instead of leaving it entirely to other departments of the company? What does the risk manager contribute to the solution of any corporate problem?

There is no unanimity among the experts on this. When risk managers ceased to be merely corporate buyers of insurance and began to recommend other treatment of risks, they became involved in changes in procedures within the corporation itself, such as improving the loss prevention technique or facilities. How far should they go?

A group of experts on the subject has said that corporate risk managers should involve themselves as much as possible in virtually any corporate situation where there is a discernible possibility of loss. On the other hand there are those who would restrict the corporate risk manager to the handling of insurable risks. To my mind there is a middle ground which should be perfectly acceptable to both schools of thought and compatible with both. All students of risk management will agree that, if insurance can be purchased for a peril, the corporate risk manager is always charged with evaluating the economics of buying this insurance. Furthermore, a fairly new definition of insurance terms it, "the pooling of risks on a voluntary basis through the use of intermediaries." Thus, the risk management department must have added responsibility over and above merely buying insurance. The department must become actively interested in all risks to which the corporation is subject if those risks are capable of being pooled in any way.

It matters not that, after due analysis, the corporation decides not to join with others subject to the risk in pooling the risk through the conventional insuring mechanism, or industrywide captive insurers or any other form of risk pooling through intermediaries.

Adapting to Swift Changes

Conditions within the corporate climate are changing with lightning-like rapidity. These changes come faster and faster as technology advances. Thus a risk which can be pooled today might well be best self insured tomorrow, and still later might better be pooled. Doesn't this define the speciality which the corporate risk manager is uniquely qualified to provide the corporation—namely, the expertise on this pooling capability, whether through the conventional insurance market or by other means?

As an aside, I am still haunted by a risk-pooling decision I was involved in some years ago. In the mid-1950s the scheduled airlines, painfully aware of the strangulating nature of work stoppages, were seeking a way to pool the financial losses that resulted from these stoppages.

The corporate insurance managers of the airlines, which included me, were asked about the possibilities of insuring this risk. To a person, we all advised that the risk could not be pooled. The general counsels of the airlines refused to accept this advice. They eventually developed the airline revenue sharing pool. The principal architect of this pooling arrangement went on to become his company's president.

Exception to the Rule

A few paragraphs above I said that all students of risk management will agree that, if insurance can be purchased for a peril, the corporate risk manager is always charged with evaluating the economics of buying this insurance.

I suspect that this statement will not go unchallenged. This is partly because the word "insurance" is sometimes used to describe what is really a tax. And it is partly because of certain insurance programs that have been developed within corporations.

For example, state unemployment insurance is really a tax. And most corporations handle it as a tax, with the corporate tax department administering it.

A good example of the second exception to my statement is title insurance, which protects the corporation against loss from defective conveyances of real estate which the corporation has purchased. The corporate real estate manager, or counsel almost always buys title insurance, instead of the risk manager. The customary reasons for this are:

- The coverage is highly specialized. It is not sold through the conventional insurance market with which the risk manager is most familiar.
- The basic service provided by the title company is title searches and related services, rather than actually absorbing losses. But, since the title insurance is only a small part of the whole title responsibility, it is only logical for it to be handled at the same time.

There may be two reasons for such a situation. The first is that corporate risk managers have not yet persuaded corporate management that they have enough expertise in these areas so that other managers can rely on the corporate risk department to handle these types of risks.

The second reason is that the corporate environment often still regards the corporate risk manager as the "handler" of fortuitous risks, involving bodily injury and property damage, rather than the types of risk that involve errors of omission.

Yet, one highly successful risk manager of a multibillion dollar company I know advises fellow risk managers to have a good working knowledge and interest in *all* corporate programs with the word "insurance" in them. His reasoning is simple and goes a long way in explaining his success as a risk manager. He says, "If something should go seriously wrong with one of the 'non-insurance' programs, with consequent loss or serious embarrassment to the company, top management could easily say to me, 'you're the company insurance expert, why don't you do something?' and the fact that I had no direct responsibility would not be a good enough answer."

8

Deductible Programs

One problem with writing about risk management is the wide variation among companies as to staffing and the degree of specialization of risk management.

A few years ago the Risk and Insurance Management Society, the professional organization for corporate risk and insurance managers, hired a consulting firm to study certain aspects of the speciality. The consultants found that, in the New York area, the top annual compensation for persons having the title of risk or insurance manager was eight times that of the lowest paid of the group. This suggests a wide variation in the intrinsic responsibilities of the incumbents and the problems they face.

There is also a wide variation in the number of people in the corporate insurance or risk management departments of different corporations. I have heard of giant corporations with as many as 60 people engaged in the speciality. At the other end of the spectrum is the company in which the treasurer also acts as the corporate insurance or risk management official on a part-time basis, with no specialized staff.

Although I know of no statistics on this subject, a good guess would be that there are about ten times as many part-time insurance and risk managers as there are full time ones. Since their problems are vastly different, this chapter is devoted mainly to the problems of the smaller risk management operations.

The Self Trained Risk Manager

The part-time specialist invariably is introduced to the speciality by being assigned the corporate insurance program, and not by being trained for it. Typically, this new corporate insurance "expert" will receive a folder of insurance contracts which describe the protection available to the corporation from the conventional insurance market. Few documents are less comprehensible to the uninitiated. They are difficult even to the initiated!

Our part-time specialist will probably have to accept much on faith until becoming better acquainted with the concepts, forms and terminology. It is typical that each type of insurance will be written by different insurers, each of which has its own style in presenting costs. Each must be successfully evaluated to achieve an efficient corporate risk management program.

To these complications must be added the variations in the term of insurance contracts and the consequent variation in the payments for the services provided. Insurance contracts with a one-year term are probably most common, followed by three-year contracts, with five-year contracts used on increasingly rare occasions. These differences present a correlation problem.

Virtually all corporate accounting departments will book these insurance costs on an "earned" basis. They will place in a prepaid expense account that portion of the insurance paid for but not yet earned by the insurance company. This accounting treatment makes the amounts shown as insurance expenses comparable in the corporate financial statements, whether contracted for on a one-year or a multiple-year basis.

Our part-time corporate insurance specialist could even apply a time value of money factor to these differing premium payments, although the discounts usually allowed by insurers for advance payment—usually 2.7 percent of annual premium for a three-year contract and 4.5 percent for a five-year program—purport to recognize the time-value element.

How to Treat Dividends

Far more vexatious in multi-year policies is the problem of treating dividends and other premium returns. A dividend paid to a policyholder is always earned on the term just expiring at the time the dividend is received. That's the very nature of such a payment. So it is, in effect, a retroactive payment (by the insurer, of course). The fact that it is contingent and payable at the end of the policy term mitigates against anticipating this premium return in booking the insurance costs on a net basis (gross premium less expected dividend). And booking the premium at the time it is received, if it is a significant amount, certainly distorts the accounting presentation of the period when such credit is taken.

Equally vexatious, this treatment overstates the insurance expense of the preceding accounting periods when the insurance expense was recorded on a gross basis. The careful specialist is best advised to get the insurer's opinion as to whether the dividend (or any other contingent premium return) is likely to be continued. If it is expected that it will be paid at the end of the policy term, it should be anticipated in the booking of insurance expense. If it is more likely that the dividend will not be paid, it should not be anticipated.

There are several very basic questions to which a newly appointed corporate risk specialist must obtain the answers. Should a risk be insured at all? If so, what is the justification? Should the corporation assume a deductible for a part of the risk? If so, in what amount?

Several years ago, I addressed a seminar conducted by the American Management Association for the part-time corporate insurance buyer or the newly appointed risk manager. What follows is a condensation of what I told them.

Let us use as an example, how a company decided to proceed to adopt a deductible for comprehensive dishonesty coverage. Deductibles for such coverage are fairly common. However, this company wanted a large deductible—$50,000 for any one loss, with no annual aggregate. And this is not common. Here is how the company rationalized its action.

Advisability of Deductibles

A deductible is, of course, a form of assumption of risk by the insured. We can tell whether or not a deductible arrangement makes economic sense by applying the same yardstick as we would in evaluating the assumption of any other form of risk.

A company looks for one or more of four conditions in any insurable risk to justify insuring the risk. These conditions are called the four Ss—Survival, Spread, Service and Statute.

Like all catch words, the four Ss tend to oversimplify the situation. Included in the category of Survival are those risks which, while they cannot destroy the company, could embarrass it, financially or otherwise.

The second S—Spread—applies to potential losses which, though not catastrophic, are severe enough and infrequent enough so that it makes economic sense to spread the risk by purchasing insurance to recover a large portion of the loss.

To comprehend the importance of such coverage, let us assume that this risk had not been insured and that a maximum loss occurred which now must be paid from company funds. When this loss is reported to higher company management, someone may ask, "How much would it have cost to insure this risk?" If it can be answered satisfactorily, then this spread element dictates that the company not go the insurance route.

To further illustrate this spread test, let us say the company was paying a $120,000 premium a year for full dishonesty coverage. Losses under the insured program had been averaging about 50 percent of premiums, or $60,000 a year. So the potential saving, based on past experience, was the other $60,000 a year, less what would have to be paid for the insured coverage above the $50,000 deductible. This premium turned out to be $12,000 a year. Clearly from the standpoint of the spread element, this program could stand a high loss. How the precise figure of $50,000 for the deductible was determined will be explained below.

The third S—Service—refers to what the insured receives for the premium in addition to the payment of losses. What services are received which the insured cannot economically perform?

We all agree that the service element has always weighed heavily in the fidelity aspect of a comprehensive dishonesty coverage. Yet, much of this service could be performed more economically within a company. Some aspect of this service would still be obtained, for a price of course, without insured coverage from $50,000 to $1,000,000, while the company continued to do much of the service work itself.

The final S—Statute—is any coverage obtained to satisfy a law. The federal welfare disclosure law requires the bonding of some employees so, for this purpose only, the insurer provides first dollar coverage by endorsement at a nominal premium cost.

Having run the $50,000 deductible on comprehensive dishonesty past the four Ss, it is concluded that a company could assume this risk.

Types of Deductibles

It has been said that the acknowledgement of ignorance is the beginning of learning. This applies well to the subject of deductibles. I think it wise for corporate insurance persons to listen very carefully, even respectfully, when representatives of the underwriting side suggest a change in insurance coverage being tailored for a company.

The example of a $50,000 deductible on dishonesty coverage illustrates this idea to some degree. The company started out considering a $13,000 deductible and had intended to self assume that amount. That is, it would set up no company reserve for it. A study by the insurer ultimately pointed to a $50,000 deductible. Adopting this required the company to self insure—that is to establish a reserve for payment of potentially larger losses than it cared to self assume.

My point is simply that corporations very often can and should be more flexible than the insurers in such matters as deductibles. The underwriter is undoubtedly trying to dovetail the proposed coverage into the existing set-up. The underwriter has many more factors than the company has to bring together, such as excess loss rate versus primary loss rate structure, credibility factors and even insurance limits. Permitting the insurer to be flexible very often puts money in the pocket of the insured.

Determining Deductible Size

Now let us see how $50,000 was arrived at as a deductible on the dishonesty coverage for any one loss, with no aggregate or other cumulative top-side limit.

As we saw, the company started out with a $13,000 deductible in mind. Now $13,000 was and is the maximum amount it must absorb into its expenses for any one loss under its retrospective rated compensation, auto and general liability coverages. It was reasoned that, since the company was accustomed to accepting as much as $13,000 ($10,000 loss plus 30 percent load charge) onto its books under an existing insurance program, it would not find this identical figure obnoxious under a new program.

Also, the company was actually encouraged to consider a much higher figure for a deductible, a figure in the area of $50,000. The company's bond indenture contained a provision that it might self assume (no reserve required) any insurance coverage up to $50,000 and could self insure to any amount. It intended to and did self insure its dishonesty coverage but saw no good reason to go beyond the $50,000 bond indenture self assumption limitation. Had the company felt there were cogent reasons for going beyond the $50,000 self assumption limitation it certainly would have done so.

So the size of the deductible, the figure finally settled on, originated not with the company, but with the insurer. What then was the actual rationale of the $50,000 deductible figure? It is hard to say. The suggestion that the market was best at the higher deductible was accepted without too much explanation.

The Rationale

You may ask, "How can you rationalize such a recommendation if you don't know the market?" You rationalize the deductible program offered by comparing it with the fully insured program you previously had.

You may recall that $120,000 was the annual premium paid

for full insurance and that the company had an average of $60,000 in losses each year. With a $50,000 deductible, the annual premium was reduced to $12,000. So, assuming a continuation of the existing experience, costs under the deductible program should be $72,000 or 40 percent less than the fully insured program. The $50,000 deductible is some 30 percent higher than the highest loss the company had under its fully insured program.

The company had a comprehensive dishonesty program with a $50,000 deductible for slightly over two years. The dollar savings each year, comparing its present costs with that paid under first-dollar coverages, has averaged 40 percent. A small, unmeasurable workload was added to its law department. It had been using the $120,000 a year as a ballpark figure for the first dollar premium costs. So the saving to date is in the neighborhood of $48,000 a year. A lot of lawyers' time can be bought for this.

The company also thinks it enjoys two additional benefits which cannot be measured in dollars. First, it is receiving payment of claims more promptly. For some reason, valid I'm sure, the insurers took an average of six weeks to two months to investigate and pay a claim under the first dollar coverage, no matter how small the dollar amount of the claim.

Under the self insured program, a second indirect benefit derived was increased loss prevention consciousness within the company. In the past, the company allocated the premium paid for first dollar coverage on an exposure basis. That is, on the basis of employees, employees handling money, safes, cash on hand, etc., irrespective of the losses. The company now bears its own losses up to $13,000.

Thus far, the losses have shown no substantial change either in frequency or in dollar amount under the self insured program when compared with the first dollar coverage program.

A Problem Remains

However, there is one concern. Call it the long view or the broad view. This concern stems from the sobering statistics arising from the activities against which comprehensive dishonesty insures. I believe Norman Jaspan, a well known security expert, mentioned the figure of $2 billion a year as the best estimate of the fidelity "take" in this country. Robbery and burglary trends are equally disturbing.

This is a big problem requiring a big solution. By withdrawing coverage for the first $50,000 from the insurance companies, are companies withholding support from the organizations which should and may be trying to be the catalyst, the spearhead, for the forces to combat these problems? A company may be doing this by self insuring but I don't think so. Until evidence suggests that there is more attention to these overall problems, in a manner similar to the magnificent job being done by fire insurers on the overall problem of loss prevention, the present setup will be kept.

9

Insurance Coverages for Business

Workers' Compensation Insurance

Workers' compensation is such a key element in the corporate insurance program that a fairly detailed analysis of it is in order. The coverage called "employer's liability" is generally similar to and written as an adjunct to workers' compensation coverage, so it will also be analyzed at this time.

Society has determined, through historical development of statutory law, that it is the responsibility of industry to compensate employees or their families for injuries or death incurred in the course of employment. Recourse to common law action, where employer negligence had to be proved by injured workers or their survivors as a means of obtaining reimbursement for lost income stemming from injuries, was found to result in inequities to employer and employee alike and placed an intolerable burden upon the courts.

The states therefore enacted Workers' Compensation Laws which provided for compensation without regard to the question of negligence. Today there are such laws, or their equivalents, in effect in all states of America, as well as in Canada and many other countries. The obligations imposed by these laws may be fulfilled by insuring with stock or mutual insurance companies or, in some U.S. states, all Canadian provinces and many foreign countries, by participating in state, province or national insurance pools. Self insuring this risk is often permitted if certain conditions are met.

While in most states the laws are so written that acceptance of statutory benefits is mandatory and any legal action against an employer is precluded, in a few states an employee may still reject the benefits and sue the employer. Most workers' compensation insurance policies therefore provide employer's liability protection in addition to compensation benefits.

No Amount or Limit Set

Workers' compensation insurance, whether purchased through private insurance companies or mandatory state funds, is designed to provide payment of benefits to the extent they are prescribed in the laws of the various states. For this reason, there is no amount or limit of insurance stated in the policies, except in the employer's liability section.

There are no two states with identical workers' compensation laws. The laws differ in the circumstances out of which injuries must occur to be compensable, in the types of injuries or occupational diseases covered, and in the extent of compensation prescribed. There are different ways claims are settled. In some states all employee classifications are covered, whereas in others only hazardous occupations (as defined in the statute) are subject to the compensation laws. And, unless special provisions are made in the insurance contract, the coverage will be limited accordingly.

Generally speaking, the laws provide for death benefits to survivors, benefits for permanent and temporary total disability (usually expressed as a percentage of wages up to a maximum amount), scheduled awards for permanent and partial disability (expressed as dollar amounts depending on the nature of the disability) and medical expenses. The policies further agree to defend suits brought against any employer by an injured worker, and to pay any awards made by the court, including costs, against the employer.

The perils insured against may be thought of as the payments, together with attendant expenses, which an employer is obligated to make under the workers' compensation law or by court decision as a result of death, injury or disease to an employee encountered during the operations of the business.

The Letter of the Law

Insurance coverage depends upon the letter of the various laws. Any areas of possible coverage not specified in the law are noncompensable, although regulating authorities may decide otherwise in a specific case. Certain occurrences, such as deliberate self-injury by the worker, or injury while intoxicated, are generally not covered under the laws.

The amount of compensation payable depends upon the schedule of benefits included in the statutes. The method by which reimbursement of compensable injuries is made to the employee or the employee's survivors varies in each state.

The most obvious service performed by the insurer underwriting this coverage is the handling and settlement of any compensable claim, or the defense of any employer's liability suit. The insurer may also inspect the working operations of an insured employer for the purpose of making recommendations toward eliminating unsafe conditions, thus reducing the accident rate, and thereby the cost of insurance.

Manual Rates

If the workers' compensation coverage generates a premium of less than $100,000 a year, the chances are that the corporation will have to be content with a program where the premium charge will be the manual premium plus or minus the insured's modification of that manual premium.

In certain instances this $100,000 breakpoint is applied to all casualty coverages—that is, the total premiums generated by workers' compensation and liability coverages. So, below the $100,000 premium level, there is little likelihood that any form of retrospective rating plan is available to the corporation.

Manual premium rates are compiled by the state compensation rating board or similar authority. These rates are compiled by job classification and reflect the degree of hazard inherent in each classification. The rates to be charged per $100 of payroll range from a low of a few cents (generally for clerical staff) to many dollars per $100 of payroll for employees engaged in high hazard occupations, such as structural steel workers or coal miners.

All manual premium rates are compiled in the same manner. The losses paid during the preceding years are analyzed and interpolated into the expected loss rate. Thus the expected loss rate for wet processing dairy employees might be 55¢ per $100 of covered payroll. To this expected loss rate will then be added the expense loading, which is the amount necessary to take care of all expenses, such as acquisition costs, loss investigation and adjusting costs and underwriting costs.

This expense loading is stated as cents or dollars per $100 of covered payroll. The expected loss rate, plus the expense loading, comprise the manual premium for each job classification.

Expected Loss Rate

An important ratio to remember is that which has been established between the expected loss rate and the manual premium rate. The expected loss rate is expected to equal 65 percent of the manual premium rate. This means that the manual premium rate for the wet process dairy employees will be about 88¢ per $100 of covered payroll. As we observed earlier, we assumed the expected loss rate to be 55¢ for these employees.

To encourage loss prevention, the state compensation rating authorities have developed a rate modification for each employer.

This rate modification is computed each year by comparing the employer's loss experience to the loss experience found within the job classification as a whole. If the employer's loss experience is better than the experience as a whole, the employer receives a credit modification. If the employer's loss experience is worse than the experience as a whole, the employer receives a debit modification.

This credit or debit modification is actually applied by the insurer to the corporate employer's workers' compensation premium expense. It can represent a substantial percentage increase or decrease in the total amount charged. The base period used to compare the employer's experience with the whole is the most immediate three-year period, with the year just past dropped out. This drop-out is necessary because the prior-year data are not available in time to be included in the analysis by the state compensation rating authorities.

Data Checklist

So, what is the minimum amount of data that our part-time specialist should obtain from an insurer or a broker about workers' compensation? Here is a suggested checklist:

1. Ascertain the job classifications and rates used in calculating the corporation's workers' compensation manual premium cost. As we saw, these rates can vary substantially and misapplication of them can be costly.

2. Ask: Are the classifications used congruent with the work the employees do? The use of a structural steel employee's classification in a dairy is undoubtedly the result of a clerical error.

3. Ask for as full an explanation as the insurer and broker can give on the experience modification for the corporation. The modification for the applicable year invariably becomes available for use in March or April of that year, so it must always be the subject of an adjustment to the rate used to calculate the premium at the beginning of the year. When the insurer or broker announces

this experience modification credit or debit, this is the best time to ask for a complete explanation of it.

4. Periodically review the losses charged against the company by the insurer. A periodic listing of these losses should be provided and become part of the file for use in making year-to-year comparisons of losses sustained. Obviously, if these losses are recited on a comparable basis, such a year-to-year comparison does not require any particular expertise in insurance or risk management. Such a year-to-year comparison can, however, provide valuable insight as to the expense and will rationalize the entire workers' compensation insurance expense in non-insurance terms. In making such an analysis the 65-35 percent loss-expected expense-expected ratio described above should be kept in mind.

5. Ask the workers' compensation insurer what loss prevention service is provided. And use it.

6. If your company belongs to an active and effective trade or industry association, seriously consider the association as an available source of information on loss prevention analysis. An exchange of ideas seems to be very productive when conducted along industry lines. Many trade and industry associations have formed insurance committees in which detailed aspects of the insurance arrangement, loss occurrences, and loss prevention measures are effectively discussed.

Second Injury Fund

A worker who has lost a hand, or foot or eye in an industrial accident may become totally disabled if the other member is lost in a second accident. For this reason, employers would tend to refuse to employ a partially disabled worker. To avoid such situations, most states have enacted provision for a second injury fund into law.

In these states, a worker who suffers a second loss of a member is compensated on the basis of his entire permanent disability following his second injury without regard to his pre-existing physical disability. The employer, however, has a limited liability following the second injury. This is because these second injury funds either pay the difference between the cost of the partial and permanent disability award or a total disability award or will reimburse the employer for all compensation payments beyond a specific period.

For example, an employer in New York is responsible for only the first 104 weeks of compensation benefits following a second injury if the conditions are such that the New York second injury fund will accept responsibility. The second injury fund is supported either by assessments levied on all insurance companies writing workers' compensation or, in some states, by the employer paying stipulated sums into the fund when a worker without dependents is fatally injured on the job.

A second injury fund is a special fund set up within the administrative framework of the workers' compensation system to insure that an employer who hires a physically handicapped worker, or continues the physically handicapped worker in employment will not, in the event the worker suffers a subsequent injury on the job, be responsible for a greater disability than actually occurred while the worker was employed.

Under such a system the employer pays only the benefits that are due for the second injury. However, the employee is fully protected because the fund pays the difference between what is actually received from the employer and what would have been received for the resulting condition if there had been no prior disability.

Coverage Varies

Some of the state second injury funds apply to many types of physical disabilities, others only a few. While there is no exact definition of what makes a law broad or narrow, those that cover many or most types of handicaps are called broad. Those that restrict coverage to "loss, or loss of use, of a hand, arm, foot, leg or eye" are called narrow. There is, of course, a middle ground occupied by laws that cover something more than amputations and sight losses, but not enough to make them really broad in their effect.

Second injury funds are financed in a variety of ways. A few states finance them wholly, or partially, by legislative appropriation. Most, however, require employers through their insurance premiums to underwrite the cost of the second injury fund program.

Today, some 14 states and the District of Columbia cover any previous permanent disability without limitations as to cause or type. However, nine of these jurisdictions require that the second injury, when combined with the first, result in permanent total disability. This is a limitation which greatly reduces the effectiveness of the second injury fund law, since it is estimated that less than one-tenth of one percent of all industrial accidents result in permanent total disability. Only four states fail to provide any protection to physically handicapped workers. They are Georgia, Louisiana, Nevada and Virginia.

The Minimal Test

On the "extent of disability", a certain minimal test is required before the employer's responsibility is shifted to the fund. This test is not required when the state laws cover only the loss, or the loss of use, of a hand, arm, foot, leg, or eye since these injuries by their very nature, are serious or significant disabilities.

But the experience of some states which have broad coverage shows that covering all types of disabilities, without also requiring a minimum extent of disability, provides employers and insurance companies a method by which they can avoid responsibilities that are properly theirs. It permits a shift of responsibility to the fund in which preexisting disability was in no sense an employment handicap or, conversely, when the second injury did not significantly aggravate the prior disability.

The New York system approaches the extent-of-disability problem by limiting coverage of prior disabilities to those that are likely to be a "hindrance or obstacle" to employment; and coverage of second injuries to those that result in a permanent disability that is "materially and substantially greater" than would have resulted from the subsequent injury alone.

In construing the degree of preexisting disability that will be regarded as a "hindrance or obstacle" to employment, New York requires that employers have knowledge of the handicap and, in the case of a latent and obscure pathological condition, further requires that employers must have acted in some way on this knowledge. For example, the factors prerequisite to second injury fund relief in New York are these five:

- That the employee has a preexisting permanent physical impairment.
- That the impairment is or is likely to be a hindrance or obstacle to finding or keeping a job.
- That the employer hired or continued the handicapped worker in employment with knowledge that the impairment exists.
- That the worker incurred a subsequent compensable accidental injury or occupational disease at work.
- That the resultant disability is greater than that caused by the second injury alone.

Since workers' compensation rates are based primarily on (1) the relative hazard in the employer's work and (2) the accident experience of the employer, it follows that physically handicapped workers cannot possibly affect the first factor and could only influence the second factor if they were prone to have more accidents than workers without handicaps. Research studies, however, have shown that, where properly placed, handicapped workers have an accident experience as good as, or often better than, other persons.

In summary, the scheme of second injury fund legislation is to facilitate and encourage the employment of the physically handicapped by limiting the financial responsibility of the employer at the time of an employee's subsequent injury occurring in its employment, at the same time compensating the worker for the combined disability by drawing on the fund.

The Casualty Package

Quite often workers' compensation is included in a casualty insurance package of coverages that all corporations must have. The liability coverages provide protection against claims made by third parties for bodily injury or property damage arising out of the activities of the corporation.

Note well the qualifications for bodily injury and property damage. The bodily injury qualification speaks for itself. Property damage applies to some form of physical damage to the party asserting the claim. Without the element of bodily injury or physical damage to property, the typical liability policies included in the casualty package will not respond.

Invariably there are two liability insurance contracts included in the casualty package—auto liability and general liability. Auto liability responds to claims by third parties arising out of the use of the company automobiles and trucks or vehicles driven by employees or other agents (legally speaking) of the insured engaged in the business of the insured.

General Liability

The general liability coverage, if it includes a product liability endorsement, takes care of virtually all of the other bodily injury or property damage claims to which the corporation must respond.

One significant difference between the workers' compensation coverage and most liability coverages is that the workers' is "no fault" in character, while the liability coverages, other than auto insurance in most states, are not. All the injured worker has to show to collect under workers' compensation is eligibility for the coverage under the statute and that the injury, being of an industrial nature, was also contemplated by the statute.

There is an additional feature of the liability coverages. The person suffering the injury or damage must show that, in some way, the corporation was negligent in conduct and it was this negligence which was the proximate cause of the injury or damage. It is the obligation of the insurer to conduct an appropriate investigation of the claims, defend the corporation in court where necessary and appropriate, as well as to reimburse the injured as the circumstances dictate.

The premium which insurers can charge corporations for liability coverages is much more free of state regulation or supervision than is workers' compensation coverage, even though the calculation of the premium starts in most states with rates duly filed with the state insurance supervisory authority.

The rates for auto liability coverages are in most instances the same as those applied to your automobile or mine. There is, however, an underwriting device called "schedule rating" which permits the insurer to make adjustments to the manual premium developed on these liability coverages for business activity. This schedule rating permits debits and credits to be applied to the manual premium for such factors as volume and loss prevention devices employed by the insured.

These factors are generally applied on a judgment basis, and there is more than just a hint that the underwriter's judgment may often be affected by the competitive posture in which the insurer finds itself.

When the Whole is Less than a Part

Not too long ago, the insurance commissioner of a large industrial state mentioned in a speech that he began his insurance career as an underwriter for a fire & casualty insurance company and that his job then involved doing this schedule rating of casualty packages consisting of workers' compensation and liability coverages for corporate insureds. Competition for the business was intense at the time.

The underwriting of workers' compensation coverage was quite rigid and not susceptible to the granting of credits. The ultimate result, according to the commissioner, was that it was not a novelty when application of maximum credits resulted in an overall credit on the combined coverages. That is, the total of the workers' compensation and liability insurance coverages was less than the workers' compensation coverage standing alone.

This anecdote illustrates how diverse the premium costs of these liability coverages can be. There are, therefore, few bench marks one can use in evaluating whether or not the liability insurance premium the corporate employer is being charged is proper. One such bench mark that might be kept in mind is the fact that most state supervisory authorities, when setting rates, contemplate a loss ratio of 60 percent and an expense ratio of 40 percent where these liability coverages are concerned.

It would seem to follow, therefore, that if the corporate insured's premium approximates 166⅔ percent of the losses, the premium being charged is the proper amount. This analysis would undoubtedly have to be computed over a period of time.

Auto Liability

As indicated earlier, auto liability insurance rates are applied to vehicles owned or leased by the corporate insured in a manner identical to rates applied to your car and mine. In general liability coverages, the exposures and hence the base to which the insurance is applied are the square footage of building space under control of the corporate insured, the amount of annual sales, and similar criteria which can give some approximation of the amount of risk which the insurer is assuming.

The auto liability coverage does not, of course, reimburse the corporate insured for damage to the insured's own vehicle. A substantial number of corporate insureds maintain an insurance contract providing for this risk. I would guess that, unless the corporate insured is extremely short of working capital or the fleet of vehicles in question contains some extremely valuable vehicles, this coverage cannot be justified by the usual and customary reasons for insuring any corporate risks—protecting the corporation from financial embarrassment, etc.

From this viewpoint, the physical damage risks to one's own vehicle is usually an attractive one to self insure. Unlike most of the other corporate coverages, the maximum possible loss is easy to ascertain. It is the value of the most valuable vehicle in the fleet.

The expense element takes up about 40 cents of the premium dollar. The corporate insured with the typical insurance contract is paying $1.66⅔ for every dollar of loss collected.

Lest I appear biased toward self insurance, I hasten to report that I know of at least one huge corporate insured, with a risk manager universally respected for competence and intelligence, which carries this physical damage coverage on a fleet of 3,000 vehicles. This corporate giant looks to the insurer, not for protection of its working capital, but rather for the convenience of bringing in the insurance mechanism when one of its employees has an auto accident in a company car, for damage appraisal and speedy arrangement to get the vehicles repaired and similar tasks with which the employee is probably unfamiliar.

This is as good a point as any to emphasize that there is more to the insurance contract than the risk-bearing aspect of the insurer. If the insurer provides a service to the corporate insured in addition to bearing the risk, this service must always be a consideration in evaluating the worth of the insurance contract.

Fire-Extended Coverage

The fire-extended coverage insurance contract, providing protection against loss by direct damage to the physical properties of the corporate insured, is generally a significant one in terms of protection it affords and of the premiums paid to the insurer. The fire part of this protection is one of the oldest of coverages. It began to evolve into its modern form with the impetus for protection arising from the great fire of London in 1699.

Over the years the perils recited in the extended endorsement to this policy have become included in this contract of "Fire-E.C." as it's often called. These perils are windstorm, hail, explosion, riot, riot attending a strike, civil commotion, damage from falling aircraft, vehicles (damage from) and smoke damage.

In recent years vandalism and malicious mischief are often added to the Fire-E.C. policy as additional protection. Technically, however, "V. & M. M." is not one of the "E.C." perils.

It should also be noted that the insuring clause for the explosion peril has a significant exclusion, namely, explosion if arising from steam jacketed and other pressure vessels which must be periodically inspected pursuant to federal or state law or local governmental ordinance. As we shall see later, this exclusion dovetails nicely into the coverage offered under boiler and pressure vessel insurance.

The typical Fire-E.C. physical damage insurance contract provides only for direct damage to the subject of insurance (the building, equipment, etc.). The damage must be caused, of course, by one of the perils recited in the contract. Losses of a collateral nature, such as those caused by lost production, the need to continue the payment of utilities and the pay of the permanent personnel at the facility, would not be paid under this physical damage contract. As we shall see later, these losses of a collateral nature can also be insured with a business interruption insurance contract.

The Value of the Loss

The Fire-E.C. contract has several significant features. One important aspect involves valuation and reimbursement. Fire insurers pay no more than the loss sustained by the insured.

A facility could be insured for $500,000. If, at the time of its complete loss by fire or one of the extended coverage perils, the facility was worth only $100,000, the latter amount is what will be paid to the insured. If, at the time of the loss, the facility is worth $750,000, the limit of the policy only, that is, $500,000, will be paid.

This is not such a one-way street as it might first appear to be. The insured can easily increase the limit of the policy to take care of the increased value of the facility. As for the $100,000 payment (because that was the amount of the loss) the customary procedure in fire insurance is that there will be no windfall. Even if the insured had two policies of $250,000 each on the facility and paid premium on both, when the $100,000 loss occurs, the two insurers will each pay $50,000 of it.

The Coinsurance Clause

A further possible restriction on loss payment is the coinsurance clause which, if it exists in the policy, may restrict payment for a partial loss of the facility. Assume that the fire policy has an 80 percent coinsurance clause (the percentage most often used).

This coinsurance clause requires the insured to maintain an amount of insurance on the properties at least equal to 80 percent of the properties' value or receive something less than 100 percent of the loss suffered. In the event of a total loss, the insurer will pay the face amount of the policy. Obviously, this will be less than the amount of the loss if the insured has not maintained insurance on the properties equal to the value of those properties. But what about a partial loss? If the amount of the insurance carried on the properties at the time of the loss is less than 80 percent of the value of the property, then the loss will be paid at the rate that the insured value bears to 80 percent of the actual value of the properties.

Calculating Fire Insurance Values

How are values calculated for fire insurance? For purposes of this discussion, there are three valuations. Here are the definitions of them:

1. *Actual cash value* (A.C.V.)—It is the valuation most often used by fire insurers. A.C.V. is the cost to replace a facility to its condition at the time of the loss. It involves calculating the cost of rebuilding the facility at current labor and material prices. From this replacement cost is then deducted a factor called functional depreciation. Functional depreciation is the amount of depreciation at the time of the loss and which measures the difference in value of the facility when it was new and when it was lost.

I dislike this definition—on two counts. Technically it is no definition at all, since it uses the term it is seeking to define in the definition. And I find it almost impossible to comprehend. So let's take an example.

Assume a 10-year-old building that cost $400,000 to build 10 years ago is destroyed by fire. Assume further its replacement cost at present labor and materials cost is $750,000.

The $350,000 increase in cost has been caused by inflation—the increases in labor and material. However, due to wear and tear, it would cost the insured $200,000 to bring the building up to the equal of a new building. This $200,000 is the functional depreciation.

Functional depreciation, unlike book depreciation, is not a product of elapsed time but rather of the condition, good or bad, by which a building or other facility is maintained. Its calculation is more of an engineering problem than it is an accounting problem. If it sounds complicated, it's because it is. A whole industry—the appraisal industry—is engaged in this endeavor, with specialists of their own, computers, structural engineers and the like.

The use of A.C.V. by the fire insurer to indemnify its insureds for losses has great logic behind it. The fire insurers strive mightily to put their insureds suffering losses as far as possible in the same condition the insureds were at the time of the loss.

2. *Repair and Replacement* (R & R)—Despite this laudable objective and perhaps due to the complications inherent in the A.C.V. calcu-

lations, the use of repair and replacement valuation appears to be growing. The R & R coverage is available by endorsement to the standard Fire-E.C. insurance contract.

This coverage pays the insured for the destroyed or damaged facility an amount equal to what it would cost to repair or replace the facility at current labor and material costs. In plainer words, the insured gets a new facility, or one completely repaired and equal to a new one, in place of the one damaged or destroyed.

Obviously this R & R coverage is simpler in every respect than the conventional A.C.V. coverage, since the nettlesome feature of functional depreciation is not involved either in the continuing administration of the insurance contract or in adjusting and settling the loss if it occurs.

This R & R coverage does present problems of its own. The most obvious one is the "windfall" problem, in which the insured suffering the loss receives a better facility than it had before the loss. In recognition of this, virtually all R & R endorsements require that the damaged or destroyed facility be actually repaired or replaced. If the insured decides against that, then payment is made on an A.C.V. basis.

3. *Book Value*—We have indicated earlier that functional depreciation is not the same as book depreciation. By book depreciation we mean the depreciation expense which an owner of a facility records for accounting purposes in recognition of the diminution in value of the facility with the passage of time. The annual depreciation expense is some percentage of the acquisition cost of the facility.

The offsetting entry to this depreciation expense charge is a credit to the depreciation reserve account maintained on the accounting books, and this reserve credit accumulates during the lifetime of the facility. At any given time the net book value of a facility is the difference between the acquisition or gross costs of the facility and this reserve for depreciation attributable to the facility.

This net book value figure is important to us in fire and other casualty losses to the facility. An amount equal to the net book value of the facility is the maximum amount which the owner of a damaged or destroyed facility can receive from the insurer without incurring a federal tax liability.

Put another way, it is only the net book value which the federal tax authorities recognize as the loss. If the insurance proceeds are greater than the net book value, then this excess is considered as income and subject to tax, generally on a capital gain basis.

The chances are that this tax factor presents no particular problem if the coverage is on an A.C.V. basis, since there should be at least a rough correlation between book depreciation and functional depreciation. The tax factor can indeed have a relevance if the coverage is on an R & R basis, since under this coverage, the recovery from the insurance company can be substantially in excess of the net book value.

Our part-time specialist, and indeed any risk manager, would be well advised to regard the R & R coverages as being composed of two parts: (1) the A.C.V. coverage and (2) depreciation insurance. Many insurers market R & R coverage in these two parts. There are differing justifications for these two coverages. To my mind one justifies maintaining A.C.V. coverage on the corporation's facilities by the following:

- In the event of a loss recoverable under the contract, the corporation does not suffer an uninsured loss. That is, the corporation's current profits are not charged with this loss.
- The near unanimity existing among corporate managements generally in carrying such insurance on their facilities makes any corporation look inconsistent which does not. In the event of a significant loss, a disgruntled stockholder could charge management with wasting the company's assets.

Neither of these reasons apply to the depreciation coverage. Therefore this depreciation coverage is justified because it makes money available to finance the new facility without requiring the corporation to use its working capital or other resources or borrowed funds.

Changes in Value

It is most important that all facilities be revalued periodically and any significant change reported to the insurance company. This is obvious if the company has increased its facilities by acquisitions or by constructing them. Not so obvious but equally important is that the value added to facilities by inflation should also be calculated and reported to the insurer.

Most large corporations report significant additions or dispositions to insured facilities as such changes occur and, then, generally on an annual basis, these values are "price trended." As indicated earlier there is an entire industry—the appraisal industry—which does this on a scientific basis.

There is a simplified way of approximating updated values. We start with the cost of constructing the facility and the year in which it was constructed. There are price trending tables available. These tables correlate the difference in the cost of construction between the year of construction and the present year. This is invariably given as a percentage.

Applying the appropriate percentage of increase (rarely in recent years has it been a decrease) to the cost of construction, we obtain an approximation of today's replacement costs of the facility. The table will also indicate how much this replacement cost should be reduced for each year the facility is in existence to reflect the functional depreciation. Applying this factor to the replacement cost approximation gives an approximation of the A.C.V. values.

Business Interruption Insurance

If one should happen to hear a risk manager or any other insurance practitioner speak of business interruption insurance, probably they're talking about "Fire-E.C. business interruption."

This insurance is designed to protect against loss of earnings of a plant or other facility during a period of suspension, whether total or partial, resulting from fire and other insured perils. It reimburses for lost profits, continuing expenses and extra expenses incurred to reduce the business interruption loss.

Typical of the continuing expenses contemplated by this insurance contract are taxes, interest on the mortgage and other indebtedness, salaries of key personnel, maintenance expenses, minimum fixed charges for utilities, and other fixed costs which continue during the period of time it would take to repair or replace the damaged property.

Our diligence and dispatch are expected; the policy is liable for the loss only for the time repairing or rebuilding would normally take. Once the premises are restored, or could have been, the insurance company's liability ends even though it may take additional time for the volume of sales or production to return to normal.

The policy does not reimburse for losses from reduction in the volume of sales or for loss of customers, or good will, shelf space, etc., even if these are irrevocably lost to the business. Deductibles, and there is invariably a deductible, may be recited in dollar amounts but, quite often, in "down time." That is, days or other time periods in which there is no production from the plants.

Business interruption insurance will protect the insured parties from the loss of earnings during a partial or total suspension of business when that suspension is caused by direct damage to the real or personal property caused by an insured peril. It should be noted that protection against business interruption losses is also available for losses arising from boiler and pressure vessel explosion and the so-called difference-in-condition perils (flood, earthquake, subsidence, etc.). As indicated earlier, such policies of insurance are rare when compared with coverage for Fire-E.C. perils.

Difference-in-Condition Insurance

A fairly new coverage available to the corporation for the protection of its physical properties is difference-in-condition insurance (D.I.C.). It is generally written as a blanket policy designed to protect the greater part of a company's real and personal property from perils, other than those covered under a Fire-E.C. policy contract, which are contemplated in an all risk insurance policy.

Flood, earthquake and subsidence are the principal perils involved in this D.I.C. coverage. At the time of the emergence of D.I.C. most corporations already had their properties protected against loss by Fire-E.C. Thus a Fire-E.C. contract plus a D.I.C. contract, in effect, provides all risk protection—hence the distinctive name.

Semantically, it's an atrocity. It is, however, a worthwhile form of protection for the typical corporation. Often this coverage is obtained in London, but there is now a growing U.S. market for it. The coverage is generally written on a worldwide basis. Note how all-inclusive is the coverage, as described in the following typical clause:

"(1) Real or personal property owned or used by the insured or hereafter erected, installed or acquired, including while in course of construction or erection and including interest in improvements and betterment of buildings not owned by insured.

"(2) The interest of the insured in, and the insured legal liability for the real and personal property of others in the insured's custody.

"(3) Personal property of the insured's officials and employees while on the premises of the insured."

Unlike a Fire-E.C. policy, the individual perils are not listed but rather the policy states that "this policy insures against all risks of physical loss or damage to property described herein, including the expense of removal of debris of such property damaged by an insured peril, except as hereinafter excluded."

Exclusions, therefore, are important. Typically, the following types of property are not covered under the policy: money, accounts, bills, deeds, securities, evidences of debt, notes, property in transit, watercraft, aircraft, motor vehicles licensed for highway whether or not on the insured's property, property insured under other all risk or similar broad contracts, property sold under conditional sale trust agreements or installment or deferred payment plans after delivery to the customer.

The following types of losses would be excluded:

- Perils insured under a Fire-E.C. policy.
- Infidelity and dishonesty of the insured or employees.
- Errors in design and faulty workmanship and faulty materials, unless resulting in the collapse of the property or a part thereof, or unless resulting in water damage.
- Electrical injury or disturbance to electrical appliances, devices or wiring from artificial causes or mechanical breakdown.
- Explosion or rupture or bursting of steam boilers, steam piping, steam turbines, steam engines, or flywheels owned or operated by the insured.
- Damage sustained to goods while actually being worked on and directly resulting therefrom.
- Ordinary wear, tear or gradual deterioration.
- Normal settling or shrinkage of walls, floors or ceilings.
- Nuclear reaction, nuclear radiation or radioactive contamination.
- War.
- Delay and loss of markets.

Boiler and Pressure Vessel Insurance

Boiler and pressure vessel explosion insurance is designed to protect from loss due to explosion and other abnormal effects (such as bulging) of pressure caused by the operation of boilers and by those other pressure vessels which must be periodically inspected pursuant to state/provincial or municipal inspection requirements.

Thus it is possible that a particular type of vessel is covered under this contract in a state which requires such an inspection, while similar vessels are not covered if located in another state where inspection is not required. The purpose of this seemingly inconsistent arrangement is to pass on to the insurer the responsibility for reacting to changes in legislation and for the accomplishment of state/provincial and municipal inspection. It should be remembered that a loss due to explosion, if not covered by the boiler and pressure vessel coverage, is invariably covered by the Fire-E.C. contract.

Here is a typical list of equipment items covered under this contract:

- All steam boilers, including piping.
- All auxiliary steam piping supplied from an outside source.
- All hot water heating boilers, excluding piping.
- All hot water supply boilers, excluding piping.
- All air tanks except those forming parts of small refrigerating and compressing machines.
- All hot water tanks over 15-gallon capacity or over 60 pounds pressure.

If mandatory inspection is required by state, provincial or municipal ordinance, the following are also included:

- All other fired objects, including piping if applicable.
- All unfired pressure vessels such as propane tanks.
- All refrigerating systems, brine piping included.
- All refrigerating systems containing unfired pressure vessels which require government inspection.

Normally it is a condition of the contract that all of the above equipment automatically comes under the contract of insurance at the time such items come into the insured's possession or control. In addition, other items of equipment which do not fall into any one of the above categories may be included by specific endorsement to the contract.

Defining an Accident

An accident is defined in the policy as: "A sudden and accidental breakdown of the object or any part thereof, which manifests itself at the time of its occurrence by physical damage to the object necessitating repair or replacement of the object or any part thereof."

Certain types of occurrences are not covered, such as: wear and tear; deterioration or depletion of materials due to corrosion or erosion; leakage at any valve, fitting, connection, joint or gland packing; the functioning of any safety device or protection device;

the breakdown of any vacuum tube, gas tube or brush; or the breakdown of any structure or foundation supporting the object.

Explosion in piping, too, must meet the "sudden and accidental" tests similar to those listed above. Even then, the piping is not usually insured if it is beyond the insured premises, or is exhaust piping transmitting steam to the atmosphere, or a deaerator, a feedwater heater, a receiver separator, or an accumulator.

In addition to the above perils, certain machines not of a pressure vessel type, nor required to be inspected by state, provincial or municipal requirement, may be included under this coverage by specific endorsement in the insurance contract. The perils provided against are the sudden and accidental disintegration due to centrifugal force. Examples of such machines, which may be included are chill rolls, balance wheels, and drier rolls.

Items not normally covered are explosions not caused by pressure, even if in a pressure vessel. An example would be a gas explosion in the firebox of a furnace. Fire damage, even though following a covered explosion, is not covered under this contract of insurance. Nor is an explosion, even if in a covered vessel *and* caused by pressure, if the explosion was the result of water used to put out the fire. Again, these events are normally covered under the Fire-E.C. contract.

Mandatory Inspections Provided

The mandatory inspection service is provided by the insurance company under this contract of insurance. High pressure boilers—that is, those over 15 psi—normally have to be inspected annually pursuant to state, provincial or municipal requirements. Low pressure boilers—those of 15 psi or less—have to be inspected at reasonable intervals, and at least once during a three-year policy period. Recommendations contained in the insurer's inspection reports are invariably of sufficient importance to warrant immediate compliance in order to prevent damage to property and injuries to personnel.

It is also a general statutory requirement that the initial installation of most pressure vessels be inspected by an approved inspection service before an operating permit is issued by the governmental agency involved. Insurance companies have such approval. It is, therefore, important that all installations which may be subject to these governmental requirements be reported to the insurance company at the time the installation is made. Once the installation has been reported to the insurance company, subsequent inspections are the responsibility of the insurance company without further follow-up from the insured.

Marine Insurance

Marine insurance covers vessels and goods travelling over water, as well as continued carriage of goods on land. Ocean marine insurance provides against loss for all overseas movements of merchandise. Inland marine insurance provides the same coverage for vessels and cargo if the loss occurs in inland waters.

It should be noted that the inland marine policy form is often used in a transportation insurance policy whether or not the movement is by water or by ground carrier.

Typically the merchandise is insured "against loss, damage or deterioration from any cause however and wheresoever arising irrespective of percentage, including strikes, riots and civil commotions, but excludes war risk." Invariably a companion policy is issued with the marine contract providing coverage for the war risk while waterborne or for 15 days on shore at a trans-shipping point. If the 15-day waiting period is exhausted, coverage then reattaches upon reloading on board the on-carrying overseas vessel to final port of destination.

A marine policy usually excludes loss or damage resulting from delay, inherent vice and/or loss of market, rancidity, war, capture, seizure, arrests, restraint, detainment, confiscation, nuclear incident, reaction, radiation or any radioactive contamination, strikes, riots and civil commotions.

The war risk policy usually excludes loss or damage caused by or resulting from commandeering, preemption, requisition or nationalization by government of the country to or from which the goods are shipped, seizure or destruction under quarantine or custom regulations.

10
The 'Giant' Corporation

The 1000 corporations listed in *Fortune* magazine's analysis of U.S. companies have assets of almost $1,300 billion, while the U.S. property-liability insurance industry, from which these companies buy much of their insurance, has a total of $190 billion in assets and $54 billion in policyholder surplus.

It is a fair guess that these 1000 corporations pay about $20 billion in premiums (one percent of their sales) to insure against losses due to fire, explosion, auto and industrial accidents. Of this, about $15 billion is used to take care of the actual losses arising from these corporations' activities. The remaining $5 billion is used to service these losses. We have selected these companies, not to imply a corporate elite, but because the *Fortune* analysis gives us such data as sales, assets and net worth. Through these basic figures we can estimate corporate insurance needs and expenditures.

Concentration of Risks

These commercial, insurable risks are becoming more concentrated, making it more difficult to insure them completely at full value under the underwriting rules followed by virtually all insurers. This concentration has been accelerated by improvements in the highway system, by greater economy of operating in fewer, larger locations, and by similar trends. The economies of such concentration are easy to observe. But what they do to the insurance mechanism is not so obvious.

All property-liability insurance companies have a limit to the size of a property risk they will underwrite at any one location. One huge property-liability insurer with assets of $4 billion has a per-location loss limitation of $400,000. This is typical. So we can see what such a concentration of facilities can do to the typical insurer's capacity to insure the risk without recourse to reinsurance under the limitation it imposes upon itself.

Such concentration of risk has been going on for some time

and will continue, whether it be manufacturing facilities, jet airplanes, super tankers, or high piled warehouses. Nothing is going to reverse this trend. The economies gained by concentration are too great for this process to be stopped.

Insurance Buys Survival and Service

It has been said that the two reasons for buying insurance are survival and service. This is an over-simplification, but it contains a great deal of truth. Without protection, if my well-mortgaged house in Connecticut were to burn (without insurance of course), its loss would be a financial disaster from which I would have great difficulty recovering. On the other hand, when the insurer of my ten-year-old station wagon reimburses me for a broken windshield worth $135, no element of survival is involved. It is really just providing me with a service to smooth out my cash outlay.

When I insure my house, my financial survival is involved. Somewhat in the same boat is the relatively small U.S. corporation with one or two plants, the value of which equal or exceed that corporation's annual sales.

But what about the company with assets running into the hundreds of millions of dollars, with annual sales also in the hundreds of millions and with many plants spread throughout the country, each with values constituting a small percentage of the total resources of the company? What kind of loss would have to occur to that company to cause as much havoc in that company's life as the uninsured loss of my house by fire were it to occur? It's my guess that, at the present time, many multi-million-dollar corporations insure against property losses which, in proportion to their assets, are more analogous to the coverage of my station wagon, than to the coverage on my house.

This condition may be changing. Not too long ago the treasurer of a corporate giant expressed the opinion that his company should not buy insurance at all except to obtain engineering and loss prevention services. His reasoning is interesting. He reasons that, unlike us humans, a corporation is a perpetuity. And that all large corporations are expected to pay for their own losses over a period of time, plus the insurers' expenses to service those losses. If the premium doesn't cover the loss plus expenses, the premium will be quickly increased. As Al Smith once remarked, "There is no such thing as a free lunch."

I cannot agree with the position expressed by this treasurer. However, the risk manager of a giant multi-billion-dollar complex is perhaps equally off base when he says "the insurance rates I've been quoted have never made it economically sensible for me to insure other than on a nominal deductible basis."

The Ultimate Solution?

Recently I had occasion to make a presentation to a committee of the board of the insurance company that employs me. To a list of external environmental events to which our company would be subject in the next five to ten years I included "The Financial Revolution" which was part of the title of a recent *New York Times* editorial commenting upon the merger of a large life insurer and a stock brokerage firm and the then proposed merger of American Express and still another stock brokerage firm. The *Times* expressed the opinion that "what is happening is the beginning of a reorganization of the finance industry" and that, at some future time "consumers will be able to insure a car, price an annuity, sell a house and cash a check in one office." The editorial called for legislation to permit banks to enter this "revolution," presumably including the area of property-liability insurance.

I expressed the opinion that if the banks were so permitted, it wasn't difficult to see them providing a financing package for plant and equipment that, if there were a loss or damage for most any reason, including those risks now insured, the financing would be adjusted accordingly. If so, I think it would be a mistake. To my mind the best possible arrangement to take care of insurable risks is a well structured, rather intimate partnership between parties susceptible to the risk and an entity, such as an insurer, whose interest in helping to keep losses at a minimum is maintained by the rather exclusive feature of service (and consequent reward) that the entity renders.

Because of this belief and my further belief that the insurance industry can best service its property customers by adapting certain of the pooling mechanisms that developed in the casualty area during the 1973–75 capacity crunch period, I have reproduced below part of an article I had published in 1969 in *Insurance* magazine. (There is error in this presentation which I shall comment upon at its conclusion.)

"I offer the following chart as a possible approach to corporate risk handling. It shows three levels of loss protection.

NATURE OF LOSS	ORGANIZATION WHICH WOULD TAKE CARE OF RISK AND ABSORB LOSS	SUGGESTED NAME FOR THIS LEVEL	DOLLAR VALUE OF LOSS (PER LOSS BASIS) Minimum	Maximum	DOLLAR VALUE OF LOSS (ANNUAL AGGREGATE BASIS) Minimum	Maximum
Losses which, under most insuring arrangements, a corporation of any size is expected to bear. Transferring these losses to an insurer merely results in dollar swapping between insurer and insured, with needless expense to both.	The company sustaining the loss. Self insurance reserve on corporation's own books covers severe loss and spreads it over several years of earnings.	Predictable loss level.	Up to	$500,000	Up to	$5,000,000
Severe losses which are too large for individual companies to absorb conveniently. When loss occurs, each member assessed its share. Industry-controlled committees and/or staff would monitor loss prevention and engineering effort of individual companies and would undertake substantial loss prevention research and similar activity.	The industry susceptible to the risk involved, i.e. airline industry for jumbo jets, oil industry for oil slick liability, etc.	Industry loss sharing level.	$500,000	$5,000,000	$5,000,000	$50,000,000
Truly catastrophic losses for virtually all corporations.	Conventional insurance market, probably through syndicates similar to American Marine Hull syndicate.	Insurable loss level.	$5,000,000	$500,000,000	$50,000,000	$500,000,000

Predictable Loss Level

"The first level covers losses to be taken care of by the corporation. This is not a novel idea. Who hasn't heard of deductibles? What may be novel is the suggestion that the level of losses should be quite high—high enough that, if the maximum occurs, either on a per loss basis ($500,000) or an annual aggregate basis ($5,000,000), that occurrence will be financially embarrassing to virtually all corporations except the very largest.

"However, such financial embarrassment is eliminated by setting up a self insurance reserve on the company's books. Then the financial impact of even the maximum loss of $5 million would be spread over the years used to accumulate the reserve. It is inevitable that such losses will occur, if one waits long enough. This should be recognized by the federal tax authorities. Additions to reserves, in reasonable amounts, should be deductible in calculating corporate income tax, just as premiums paid to insurance companies are deductible.

"The economies arising from this self insurance arrangement are obvious. The insured saves the difference between the insurer load charge and what it costs for loss servicing. Inspection and engineering services, formerly supplied as part of the insuring arrangement, can be contracted for separately. One aspect of self insurance is often overlooked: it generally results in better loss prevention. Being borne by the insured, the loss and financial outgo implicit in the loss comes into much sharper focus for the insured, and the employees of the insured, than if the loss were to be paid by the insurer.

"By taking care of these predictable losses, the corporation relieves the insurance industry of them. This should free up a large segment of insurance capacity for insurers to take care of the segment of the loss absorption process assigned to them.

Industry Loss Sharing Level

"The second level in the chart is somewhat novel. It is true that in Germany the equivalent of our workers' compensation has been handled by industry pools since the time that protection became available. It is also true that we are seeing the beginnings of industry pools of a loss-sharing nature. These are beginning to appear because of stark necessity—because of the near absence of insurance capacity to take care of the large volume of risks.

"There are the aircraft builder's council, several industry-owned insurers, and the protection and indemnity clubs that provide liability protection to marine insureds. Every industry with an insurance problem should explore, probably through its trade association, the possible pooling of risks within that industry. This could involve product claims, product recall, air and water pollution and high-piled warehouse destruction.

"The possibilities of effective risk pooling and loss abatement are immense. Since loss reimbursement from an industry group would begin at a high level (the chart suggests $500,000 per loss and $5,000,000 annual aggregate), the incidence at this level should be low, thus requiring a simple supervisory mechanism.

"Because the company to be reimbursed would have had to absorb a substantial share of the loss, paying members of the industry would not feel they are subsidizing a careless, loss producing member. Again, because of low frequency, it should be possible to pay any loss on a post-assessment basis, rather than on a prefunding basis. This offers a distinct advantage. Insurance companies must always prefund these high level losses. Due to the nature of this coverage, many years of premium payments can pass before a loss occurs. The inevitable loss is always many hundreds (sometimes thousands) of times the size of the annual premium.

"Despite the fact that many years of premium paying is supposed to take care of the infrequent loss, the insurance industry seems incapable of absorbing the psychological impact of this large disparity between loss and current premium. Witness the collapse of the Simmons pool, the frenetic adjustment upwards of premiums by Lloyd's and the drying up, generally, of insurance capacity on high level corporate risks.

"Loss prevention programs on an industrywide basis would probably provide more benefit to the corporate participants than the dollar economics inherent in the pooling of risk. Certainly the innate knowledge (including techniques for preventing loss by fire) as to the best, most efficient way to build and operate a fluid milk plant is to be found in the fluid milk industry. The fact that the industry would bear directly as much as $50 million of loss would act as a powerful catalyst to the industry to get the best possible operating and engineering talent to concentrate on loss prevention. (By operation of the insurance rate and classification system, the fluid milk industry bears indirectly all the fire losses of that industry, but that fact is not obvious.)

Insurable Loss Level

"We come now to the conventional insurance industry's participation in this loss pooling device described in the third level of the chart. Under the plan recommended here, the insurance industry would be the intermediary for the pooling of losses involved in high level risks. There are, of course, the genuinely catastrophic risks which occur in excess of a per occurrence limitation of $5 million and an annual aggregate of $500 million.

"I asked an officer of a larger insurer to comment on the concept embodied in the chart. His answer, predictably enough, was that the insurance industry could not successfully handle the high level, catastrophic losses without receiving the premium volume from the lower level losses. I believe this line of reasoning is utterly fallacious. It suggests that the solution to the problem of pooling high level, catastrophic losses rests in attempts to have those subject to lower level risks subsidize, directly or indirectly, the handling of the high level losses. That is the quickest way I know of to socialize the industry.

"A great student[1] of the commercial and industrial picture has said that 'the solution to a problem rests *in* the problem.' The solution to the high level, catastrophic risk problems rests in the proper perception, evaluation, pricing and pooling of these risks among those susceptible to the risk.

"I suggest the insurance industry be used as the intermediary. This is being done today, but in a most unsatisfactory manner. There is the capacity shortage and the repeated failures, at renewal time, to fill out completely those excess insurance contracts involving high level corporate risks. In justice to the insurance industry, however, and in recognition of the substantial changes inherent in the plan herein proposed, the ground rules of obtaining and maintaining this insurance would have to be changed drastically.

Long Term Contracts

"The first such change of ground rules is to recognize that such risks are completely and absolutely outside the scope of the usual and ordinary underwriting criteria. Such losses occur sporadically and with great unpredictability.

"So it is impossible to put a precise figure on the cost of protection from these risks. This has to be recognized both by insurer and by insured. One way to recognize it is to write these contracts for a long period—say five years, or even ten. Another approach would be to provide for an open end arrangement on premium payments. Even a retrospective charge equal to 100 percent of the annual premium charge on one of these excess insurance contracts would be a minor adjustment to absorb in a corporate insurance program. Yet it could give the relief needed by the insurer in a bad loss year.

"Still another aspect which insurer and insured should pursue together is to convince the income tax authorities of the certain, yet sporadic nature of these losses. An intelligent recognition of

---

[1] Mary Baker Follett

this by the tax people should permit the insurers to keep virtually all of the premium accepted for this risk in an incurred, unreported reserve, free of tax for as long as ten years.

"So it is obvious that the insurers and the multi-million-dollar corporate insureds need each other, but in substantially different roles than at the present time. Much planning, effort and coordination, accompanied sometimes by considerable stress, will be needed to bring about these changes.

"There is no doubt that they have to be made. The only alternative for corporate insurance or risk management is that it will be supplanted by some other specialty within the corporation. For the insurers, the alternative is out and out replacement by some entity, possibly by government, more suited to the needs of those being serviced."

Corrections to Note

The first, most obvious correction of the above is that there is no longer a shortage of insurance capacity; as of this writing there is a capacity glut in most insurance lines.

The three-year "up" cycle, which was the typical period of such activity is now in its fifth year with no sign of abatement. The plan suggested is designed to go beyond cycles and, to my mind, still has validity.

The second correction is that the self insurance reserve is now no longer permitted under FASB No. 5, the effect of which is described more fully in another chapter of this book. The effect of a self insurance reserve can probably still be obtained by forming a captive insurer. But, in the absence of a rather severe shortage of insurance capacity, the necessary impetus to form such a captive is not present.

11
The Conventional Insurance Market

For our purposes, the conventional insurance market is defined as those insurers and the intermediaries they use—the insurance agents and brokers—who offer themselves to the public as accepters of insurable risks. It includes all insurers admitted to do business in the U.S., whether "agency" or direct writers (whose hallmark is that they deal directly with the insured party rather than through an agent or broker). It includes, of course, Lloyd's of London and other "alien," i.e. non-U.S., insurers with whom U.S. corporations do business, and, in recent years, a growing number of captive insurers have been accepting non parental or third party risks.

These insurers can be stockholder owned, or organized as a mutual or a reciprocal (often described as a nonincorporated mutual insurer). Interestingly enough the Lloyd's insurers, organized as partnerships, are called syndicates in accordance with British word usage.

The conventional insurance market does *not* include captive insurance companies, whether owned by companies or industrial groups, whether domestic or offshore, if the captive confines its writings to those of its parent. Nor does it include the trusts organized by non-insurer organizations to service pensions and similar employee benefits. Of course, it does not include any form of self-insurance program which a company might organize to take care of its own risks. And it does not include those inspection, engineering and loss handling companies which have come into being to assist the corporate self insurer.

Impressive Characteristics

Dollar-wise, what are the dimensions of the conventional market? No one really knows with any degree of accuracy and experts would disagree if they were to guess. The one, accurate statistic describing a substantial part of this total market is supplied by

A. M. Best & Company of Oldwick, N.J., on those insurers comprising the U.S. "admitted" (i.e., licensed in at least one U.S. state or the District of Columbia) market. In the latest figures available, Best's reports that there are some 1,400 plus insurers in this market with assets of $187 billion and policyholder surplus of $54 billion. Using this surplus, $91 billion of net premiums were written during the last year reported.

To these domestic insurers operating on an admitted basis, we must add the considerable influence of the Lloyd's of London insurers, who are admitted as reinsurers and, as such, not included in Best's figures, the British non-Lloyd's market and other alien insurers (such as Swiss, German and Japanese) operating in the United States on a non-admitted basis. The dimensions of this alien, nonadmitted market cannot be accurately calculated.

The Lloyd's of London organization, which operates largely on a nonadmitted basis insofar as directly written premium is concerned (it's an admitted insurer only in the states of Illinois and Kentucky) publishes data which indicate that its syndicate partnerships have premium writings for business arising in the U.S., which average in an area in excess of a billion dollars annually. The estimate most often heard of the resources standing behind these Lloyd's resources is in the area of $2 billion. The partners (called "names") that comprise the Lloyd's syndicates emphasize, with justifiable pride, that their entire personal fortunes stand behind their underwriting activity.

Billions in Trust Funds

Another measurement of the influence of this alien, insurance market is available in the amounts of money contained in the so-called trust fund accounts of these insurers. These are monies which these insurers have placed in U.S. financial institutions to assure their availability for use in discharging their obligations. These monies run into billions of dollars. Best's reports that there was over $3 billion in the Lloyd's trust fund maintained in the U.S. as of December 31, 1980.

75% of All Insurable Risks

The proper functioning and cooperation of the conventional insurance market are essential to the success of a corporate risk management program. Some would say that it is *the* essential to such success. It is probably an accurate guess that 75 percent of all insurable risks or exposures to loss to which the typical corporation is subject are still transferred to the conventional insurance market.

In the early 1970s, even though insurance capacity offered by the conventional insurance market was quite plentiful, some corporate risk managers began to retain the lower level "first dollar" property losses. This was done by writing the insurance contract with a deductible. By this arrangement the insured agrees to absorb some part of losses, sometimes on an annual "aggregate" basis—the total of loss occurring during a given year—but more often on a "per occurrence" basis. The aggregate coverage could be, and often is, superimposed over the per occurrence insured arrangements.

Thus, if the total losses in a given year on a per occurrence basis (whether or not these per occurrence losses are insured) exceeds an amount agreed upon, say $5 million, the aggregate insurer is responsible for losses exceeding this agreed $5 million amount. Total reimbursement under this aggregate coverage is, of course, for an agreed amount. In comparison to the total risk involved, the risks so retained were modest. In the area of losses from third party liability, there was even less self insurance of loss by corporations. This was probably because specialized personnel were needed to investigate, adjust and settle liability claims, no matter how small the amount.

In workers' compensation, there were some employers with huge numbers of employees who were and had been self insuring, especially if many employees were concentrated in a few locations. But there was still great reliance on the conventional insurance market to take care of their workers' compensation losses on a conventional basis—that is, with an insurance contract in which all elements of adjusting loss were largely in the hands of the insured.

Capacity Crunch Impact

Two events then occurred which greatly affected the conventional insurance industry and, as a consequence, how the risk manager was to do the job.

The first was the 1973–75 insurance company capacity crunch, during which many large risks became increasingly difficult if not impossible for the conventional insurance market to accommodate. The first coverage to feel distress was medical malpractice liability, followed closely by hospital professional liability coverage and then by products liability coverage for manufactures of machinery, tools and similar items.

All of these coverages had the common attribute of a long tail—that is, a large volume of late maturing losses. The possibility of loss would often not even be reported to the insurer (or the insured party for that matter) for as long as five to twenty years. Before the insurance capacity turned progressively to adequacy and then to a glut, many risk managers of large and not-so-large companies found it very difficult to obtain insurance coverage at reasonable or "affordable" rates.

The second event that affected the insurance market was the promulgation in March, 1975, of FASB Standard No. 5, entitled "Accounting for Contingencies," by the Financial Accounting Standards Board, an organization comprised of accountants in public practice whose pronouncements are controlling in the accounting profession.[1]

FASB No. 5 Impact

Standard No. 5 had a marked effect on corporate activity in self insurance. It stipulated that an estimated loss from "an existing condition . . . involving uncertainty as to possible . . . loss" could and, indeed, should be recognized as an expense on a company's books only if it is probable that the loss had actually been incurred at the date of the financial statements and that the amount of the loss could be reasonably estimated.

This had the effect of requiring corporations whose statements must be certified by a CPA to eliminate most of their self insurance reserves on the company's books, at least if those reserves were for property losses since these reserves are almost always based on the company's past loss experience and not on the fact that a loss had actually occurred. Property losses have a very short tail. They are usually settled soon after they occur.

The FASB 5 standard also had a serious impact on insurance companies with public stock ownership who had set up contingency or catastrophe reserves to cover such severe losses as a major hurricane every five years, with 20 percent of the loss charged to the reserve each year. FASB 5 required such companies, who were

---

[1] Statement of Financial Accounting Standards Board (FASB) No. 5, Accounting for Contingencies, March, 1975, published by Financial Accounting Standards Board, Stamford, CT 06905.

required to provide a clean accountant's certification of their financial statements, to eliminate these reserves from their balance sheets and to return the credits contained in them to the income statement.

The liability and workers' compensation self insurance programs were not as much affected, since in most large corporations there is generally a high loss frequency. If this loss frequency is combined with a long tail and there is a creditable way to calculate the probable amount of the loss, continuation of the self insurance program was possible. And many corporate self insurers continue to do so.

Views of the IRS

It should be noted that what we have discussed above involves only the treatment of self insurance expenses and self insured reserve items on the financial statement of the corporation and not the federal tax aspects of these items. As uncertain as these items are in the accountant's treatment of them on the company's books, the federal tax aspects are even more uncertain.

The Internal Revenue Service has always looked with disfavor on permitting a tax deduction for most kinds of reserves. Self insurance reserves are no exception. For many years the IRS maintained that there was no deductibility for the reserve per se. That is, the Service would allow a deduction only for paid losses in a self insured program.

Some time in the early 1960s this policy was relaxed a little. For a while, at least in some IRS districts, a deduction was allowed if there was an unequivocal obligation by the employer to pay a claim and if the amount of the claim was certain. But in the district where I was then employed, there was little loosening of the strict concept that the loss had, in effect, to be paid. There were several years when the tax department of my employer found that hundreds of thousands of dollars of self insurance reserves had been set aside, but not once was it found that an unpaid loss should be claimed for tax purposes. The IRS held, for instance, that a reserve set up to pay a widow her benefit under workers' compensation because of the death of her husband by industrial accident was not "an unequivocal obligation to pay," because the statute provided that, if she remarried, the amount of the reserve could be reduced or eliminated.

In 1975 the Crescent Wharf case provided a basis for the tax deductibility of unpaid loss reserves if "liability was certain" and there was a reasonable way to determine that liability. Note the similarity between this rationale by the court and the determination made by the accountants in FASB 5. We shall continue this discussion in other chapters in which we go into greater detail on self assumption, self insurance, and the captive insurance company concept.

Why Do Big Corporations Insure?

I devoted one Sunday afternoon to estimating the amount spent on corporate insurance premiums and on systematic self insurance reserve additions by that segment of American corporations large enough to encompass the entire aspect of corporate risk management. After consulting the *Statistical Abstract of the U.S., Best's Aggregates and Average* and *Fortune's* lists of the largest U.S. corporations, it is my guess that the 4000 corporations which employ risk or insurance managers have about $2,000 billion in annual sales, about $1,400 billion in assets, and spend, one percent or $20 billion a year for corporate insurance within the parameters described above. And probably not more than one percent of this amount, $200 million, is spent annually on self insured programs. If these empirical figures are correct we wonder why American corporations with assets and net worth many times more than that enjoyed by the casualty insurance industry, look to that industry for protection against loss. In other words why do these huge enterprises insure at all?

Several reasons come to mind. One reason is the strong tradition among commercial and industrial firms to insure their risks. The tendency to conform is present among us all in varying degrees. If anything, this tendency to conform is more prevalent in large corporations than among the population generally. All of us are bound by that ever present legal device, the reasonably prudent man rule as applied to our specialty, whether we are risk managers or financial executives or chief executive officers. Perhaps it wasn't intended by its propounders, but this common law legal concept, purporting to describe an acceptable rule of conduct, places the burden of explaining such (non conforming) conduct on the innovator. Conformity is on the side of the status quo.

The Added Services

Another reason why large firms insure risks is that they thereby obtain many services offered by insurers in addition to actually bearing the risk. These other services are loss adjustment, investigation and abatement.

Thus fire insurers specializing in insuring large corporate risks will invariably offer inspection service. This service provides periodic inspection of the insured properties to uncover fire hazards and other potentialities for loss. When a company is erecting a new building, fire insurers will recommend a design that will minimize fire loss, as well as fire protection equipment to be installed.

Serving as Investigator

Still another service which insurers provide is to investigate whether the insured is responsible for the loss and negotiate the amount of settlement as far as third party liability and workers' compensation coverages are concerned. It is inevitable that a corporation of any size is going to have claims made against it for auto accidents with the corporate fleet and other accidents in corporate activities.

Someone has to provide these services. By buying insurance, the corporation gets the services along with the protection.

Forced to Bear Risks

The 1973–1975 insurance company capacity crunch has irrevocably changed the manner in which the corporate risk manager operates. This is particularly true in large corporations—the ones on *Fortune*'s lists—and other companies with difficult product liability or professional liability risks.

Because of the difficulty in obtaining insurance through the conventional insurance market, the end effect of the capacity crunch was that corporations were forced to bear fortuitous risks to a greater degree than before. This was done mainly by taking much larger deductibles on coverages which lend themselves to the deductible approach.

The crunch also gave a powerful impetus to the captive insurance company movement which had previously been confined largely to insuring the risks of the parent corporation's non-U.S. activities. Another impetus was the emergence of specialty insurers, most of them rather small. These specialty insurers led the way to an unbundled approach (without services) and other innovations in the coverages themselves.

Certain coverages lend themselves to different forms of retention by the corporation. First are the property coverages—fire, extended coverages, and other forms of two-party insurance. Two-party insurance is insurance with two parties to the contract, the insurer and the insured. This is in contrast to third-party insurance where, in addition to the insurer and the insured, there is another party, which might be a member of the public, as in the case of liability insurance, or a company's employees, as in workers' compensation.

There is no law that requires a corporation to insure its property against loss by fire or windstorm, or its vehicles against damage or theft. But there is indeed a law in virtually every state which requires an employer to protect its employees from injury by industrial accidents, either through the insuring process or in the almost equally complicated process of becoming a self insurer. Not surprisingly, therefore, it was the property insurance coverages that became the subject of large deductibles during the capacity crunch, to reduce the strain on the existing capacity and to permit the corporation to save money by retaining this risk.

Excess and Surplus Lines Insurers

During the capacity crunch there was much more use of the excess and surplus lines insurance industry. This industry specializes in the type of insurance which came into greater demand when the use of deductibles began to spread. Excess insurance is that coverage which comes into play at the point above the amount of the deductible. This might be $1000 per accident or, in some instances, as high as $100 million. Surplus line insurance, which may also be excess insurance, is not necessarily exclusive to that type of coverage. Surplus line is so called because it can be offered in a given state or other jurisdiction only if the existing authorized insurance market does not offer the coverage. If the risk is a type permitted by the laws of the state, it can also be covered by surplus line if there is not enough market available to accommodate the amount of coverage desired.

The surplus lines broker must find out and be able to prove that the coverage desired is not available in the state or other jurisdiction through the authorized market.

If it is a coverage which is not permitted under the insurance code of the state involved, then obviously it is surplus line by its very nature. Lloyd's of London operates almost exclusively in this surplus lines area. This surplus lines market and its workings are highly sophisticated. In most states the broker involved must have a special surplus lines license and must be cognizant of the surplus lines market; where it is, how it operates and the procedures followed in that market.

The "consent to rate" laws found in the insurance code of some states are somewhat analogous to the surplus lines market in ultimate effect, even though the operation is vastly different. The party who has a risk which he wants insured in a state where there is a consent to rate law feature in the insurance code can, through this device, actually agree to pay a higher premium than the rate schedule provides. In this way, the insurer admitted in the state can accept the risk for the higher premium.

Assigned Risk Plans

The assigned risk pool and other types of insurance arrangements, formed pursuant to state statute and designed to provide insurance to persons or corporations who could not otherwise obtain it in the normal insurance market, is another device which, strictly speaking, is part of the conventional insurance market. By these assigned risk plans the state requires that the insurers licensed to do business in the state, and for the line of coverage involved, accept the risks of these parties who otherwise would not be able to obtain insurance. Insurance through these various state-mandated plans is invariably obtained through a broker in a manner identical to insurance obtainable on a normal basis through the conventional insurance market.

Specialty Insurers

The specialty insurers that came into prominence during the capacity crunch were generally small operations. They did not offer in-house loss adjusting, inspection, engineering and other services offered by the large insurers. These specialty insurers, including the one I am associated with, in effect, offer risk managers the opportunity to insure the corporate risk without providing all the ancillary services. The insurer may, if the risk manager wishes, contract for the services of a loss adjuster or an engineering organization.

Again, when the insurance capacity moved back to an adequate level and then to a glut, the large insurers, to protect their market or for other reasons, began to offer this "unbundled" coverage as well. This ultimately enhances the position of and the ability of the corporate risk manager to control the company's program in greater detail.

Flexibility also exists in handling liability insurance. This is done by assuming deductibles to whatever degree the risk manager wishes or can negotiate with the insurer. Here again, the unbundling of services offered by the specialty insurer became available from the very large insurers.

Not as easy was workers' compensation coverage. The crunch did, however, increase the number of fairly large corporations who became licensed to self insure with stop loss coverage on the corporation's risk, since it is in all states unlimited liability so far as the risk of loss is concerned.

Surety Treated as Insurance

Surety coverage, while technically not insurance coverage but rather a form of guarantee, is treated by corporate risk managers as a form of insurance. It has not usually been subject to the deductible approach, perhaps, because it does not represent a substantial outlay to the corporation when compared to that of liability or workers' compensation, except in a few industries such as construction.

Surety is that coverage which provides that one party, the surety, agrees to answer for the loss on the default or failure of another party.

One billion-dollar company has surety coverage in which the surety, with great solemnity, agrees to reimburse the farmers of upstate New York who sell their milk to this company, if the company should default due to insolvency. An anomaly arises from the fact that the insurer-guarantor has a surplus of $80 million, while the insured corporation has a net worth of approximately a billion dollars. The $80 million is about the amount the corporation holds in cash and cash equivalent funds.

A further anomaly in this coverage arises from the fact that, if the surety should have to pay off any of the farmers on behalf of the corporate giant, it has an unequivocal right to collect from the corporate giant whatever it has paid out. Assuming the possibility of the corporate giant going broke is insignificant, the transaction is risk-free where the surety is concerned.

Why then is this coverage bought? The answer is simply that this surety bond is required by a state statute if one buys milk from the farmers of New York State! There is no way, short of repealing the law, to eliminate the need for this anachronistic coverage. Although the coverage just described is an extreme example, this anachronistic element is found in enough coverages in corporate insurance to make a detailed study of it seem, at times, like a study of *Alice in Wonderland.*

Minimizing the Losses

One succinct phrase, often heard, fairly well describes the ultimate objective of the corporate risk manager. It is, "to minimize losses, particularly the small ones, and stabilize the large ones." The obvious way to minimize losses, particularly the small ones, is to emphasize loss prevention, thus reducing losses to a minimum, and to make sure that, when losses do occur, they are adjusted and settled as expeditiously and economically as possible.

As for the large losses, the first thing to note is that they are inevitable. Perhaps the most significant aspect of the risk manager's job is to attend to and study the large loss possibilities. It can certainly be the most dramatic. The risk manager will strive mightily to reduce the probabilities of loss, but will also go further. The risk manager's attitude or philosophy can best be illustrated by Murphy's Law which states: "If anything *can* go wrong, it will."

The careful risk manager, aware that the large loss can occur, will have some plan to ameliorate as much as possible the effect of the loss. A most obvious amelioration, of course, is to have provided for its reimbursement through insurance. In considering and preparing for the large loss, the careful risk manager might do well to adopt the philosophy implicit in Pascal's great argument as to why mankind should adopt, as a working hypothesis, the concept that there is a hereafter. If there is a hereafter, the adherent to Pascal's argument has observed all of the amenities; if there is no hereafter then it doesn't make any difference!

Attitudes Before and After Loss Occurs

The careful risk manager will also be aware of two attitudes virtually all human beings have toward a large loss of a fortuitous nature and particularly one which could, even though remotely, have been prevented or otherwise stabilized. Before the loss occurs all of us—risk managers, the plant or division management that must bear the continuing cost of loss prevention equipment or paying insurance premiums, and top management—have a tendency to emphasize the cost of stabilizing the loss. And we question the need for continuing these expenditures. We also tend to deemphasize the potential effects of the loss.

But after the loss actually occurs, we all have a tendency to emphasize the effects of the loss. We can't help but do so because the effects are vividly in front of us. If this latter attitude should evolve to a condition of second guessing, it is the risk manager who usually will be on the defensive. This dual attitude is understandable. The occurrence of a significant loss is a traumatic experience, with all of the reevaluations implicit in sustaining a trauma. It is the wise risk manager who is sensitive to this dual attitude.

Speaking Up

This discussion leads logically to the question of what does the risk manager do when a substantial risk within the corporation has been identified, and the risk manager believes it should be insured or otherwise stabilized, but higher corporate management does not agree. This is often a topic for discussion when risk managers get together. One answer goes something like this, "we're not insured but I'm covered; I've written my boss a memorandum that I think we should be."

My own view is that while such a memorandum might not do any harm, it probably won't help much either if, through the workings of Murphy's Law or for other reasons, the large loss occurs. Higher management could well decide that a greater degree of articulation and persuasiveness on the part of the risk manager would have resulted in the desired stabilization of risk having been accomplished in time to prevent the traumatic loss.

Two conclusions can be drawn from this discussion. One is that the risk manager, in the situation described above, should consider that having formed the opinion that some aspect of risk stabilization is lacking, this lack is unfinished business within the company and every opportunity available should be taken to persuade the company to this point of view. The second conclusion is rather obvious yet bears articulating: The risk manager's success and continued career is, itself, subject to a host of fortuitous events, over which there is little or no control. The point is that the risk manager is in the business of fortuitous risks.

For the risk manager to be able to make an intelligent recommendation whether to insure a given risk, or to self insure, it has to be determined what the corporation is buying for the insurance premium paid. Is the premium being paid in line with the risk being transferred? What services are included? What responsibilities has the corporation contracted to perform for the benefit of or at the request of the insurer? What should be the amount of the deductible, if any?

12

The U.S. Insurance Exchanges

This chapter was contributed by my son Edward P. (Ned) Lalley and is provided with permission of Fred S. James & Co., for whom he served as a summer intern during which time he researched this subject.

The concept of the insurance exchange started in the late 1600s in a London coffee house. It was a place for shipowners to pool their money to insure that, in case of the loss of a ship, money could be drawn from the pool to cover the loss. It came to be known as Lloyd's of London, which grew into today's sophisticated multimillion-dollar central marketplace for risk managers.

The many individual members of Lloyd's, known as "names," are highly financed and capable of sharing in virtually any insurable risk from conventional fire to multibillion-dollar oil tankers, in addition to the more exotic risks, such as Betty Grable's legs and Liberace's hands.

Lloyd's success has been further enhanced by the relatively lenient regulatory stance of the English authorities and by the fact that each name at Lloyd's is subject to unlimited liability.

Now, nearly three hundred years later, the concept of the insurance exchange has been transplanted to the United States. In 1979 the New York Insurance Exchange was established.

Two basic reasons were behind it:

1. The U.S. insurance market loses approximately $1.5 billion in premiums a year to Lloyd's.
2. U.S. insurance brokers were finding some difficulty in gaining direct access into the Lloyd's market.

The N.Y. Exchange

Although the New York Insurance Exchange resembles Lloyd's in many respects, there are also some notable differences, as revealed in the following description of the New York facility:

The New York Insurance Exchange will provide a central insurance market similar to Lloyd's of London. It will have a trading floor where underwriting syndicates will offer:

1. Reinsurance of all kinds.
2. Direct insurance of all kinds from outside of the United States.
3. Risks which have been submitted to and certified as having been rejected by the Free Trade Zone. The Free Trade Zone is a classification of risks that are exempt from policy and rate requirements with respect to large commercial risks exceeding $100,000 in premiums.

An underwriting member submits initial paid-in capital of $3,550,000 to be permitted to write all kinds of insurance other than life, accident, annuities or health. To write all kinds of insurance, an underwriter produces paid-in capital surplus of $6,550,000.

The initiation fee for a broker and underwriting member is $10,000, plus annual dues specified by the Board of the Exchange.

The Free Trade Zone Concept

The concept of the Free Trade Zone, as well as the New York Insurance Exchange, came about through an act of the New York legislature. The Free Trade Zone was seen as the first step in easing the cumbersome regulations of the New York Insurance Department.

When the concept of the Exchange came along, many New York insurance interests insisted on the Free Trade Zone provision for the writing of direct business in the Exchange. The reason was simple. The insurance companies would not permit non-regulated competition from the Exchange. The New York insurers, who bear the costs of regulations, fair plans and assigned risk pools, felt it would be unfair not to get the first opportunity to write New York direct business.

This may be a valid point. However, there are negative aspects to be considered. The limitation of the Free Trade Zone may severely hamper the Exchange's chances of success. Without the unrestricted ability to write direct insurance, as well as reinsurance, the Exchange may never achieve a dominant status similar to Lloyd's, which has no such restrictions.

At this writing a bill is presently being considered by the New York Legislature to deal with these restrictions. It reads:

"Direct insurance of all kinds on risks located in the United States other than in this state, provided that such risk qualifies for placement pursuant to the excess and surplus lines requirements of the jurisdiction in which the risk is located, the superintendent shall have the authority to permit the exchange and/or its syndicates to take such steps as may be necessary to qualify as an excess and surplus lines insurer in such jurisdiction."[1]

Some of the major companies and brokers involved in the Exchange are AIG, INA, Marsh & McLennan, Continental Corp., Johnson and Higgins,Allianz Insurance and Crum and Forster.

The Exchange started slowly but is growing. By September 1981 25 syndicates, 52 brokers and 21 associate brokers had become members of the Exchange, and premium volume was $90.3 million. Low participation has been attributed mainly to the limitations of the Free Trade Zone. However, there are many uncertainties concerning the Exchange, including tax advantages, antitrust regulation, and the need for the Exchange itself.

Tax Accounting Considerations

These factors will be crucial to the Exchange's success. The majority of the participation and capitalization of the Exchange will come from the insurance industry. However, it is hoped that there will be participation by non-insurance industry syndicates because of the investment opportunity presented by the Exchange.

The Exchange is designed to let entities set up their syndicates on the Exchange as partnerships. This would allow corporations to set up syndicates with limited liability while still giving them a tax advantage—a strong incentive to invest in the Exchange.

Another tax ruling that the Exchange is awaiting deals with accounting procedures for syndicates. Syndicate partners would have to be allowed, like casualty companies, to use statutory accounting procedures to determine their taxes or underwriting income. Under statutory accounting procedures, acquisition expenses, such as commissions to agents or brokers and premium taxes, are immediately charged against the current year's operations, whereas the revenue

---

[1] State of New York, Senate Bill 3526, February 1981. This bill was passed in February 1982.

or premiums earned are systematically put into earnings on a pro-rata basis. This does not conform with generally accepted accounting principles, because expenses are not properly matched with revenues.

Statutory accounting principles allow insurance companies to deduct loss reserves as soon as they are established, even though money may not be paid out in claims until several years later—in effect a tax deferral. This is an advantage that would make the Exchange an attractive investment. It has been speculated that a syndicate might be able to produce both tax exempt income and tax losses simultaneously.

Is the NYIE a Profitable Investment?

Judging by ratios common in the casualty industry, a $100,000 investment might produce $300,000 annually in premiums written. This is in keeping with the 3 to 1 rule. We will assume that $200,000 is earned during the first year. Expenses typically run to about 25 percent of premiums written, or $75,000. This leaves a cash flow of $125,000 for the year. The statutory accounting procedures allow loss reserves to be deducted from income before taxes. The loss reserve can fluctuate considerably, but 70 percent of premiums earned, or $140,000 would be a good estimate. In a new business, only about 10 percent of that might actually be needed to pay claims during the year.

The syndicate member would thus have revenues, but expenses and loss reserves of $215,000 ($75,000 plus $140,000) which would provide underwriting losses of $15,000 which could be used to offset taxable income. For a person in the 70 percent tax bracket, this would generate $10,000 in tax savings. If the syndicate's cash were invested in municipal bonds or other tax free investments, it might easily produce in addition a 15 percent return on the $100,000 investment. The cash the investor would actually receive, however, would depend on what the syndicate manager decides to distribute.

If the syndicates cannot be taxed like an insurance company, the member in the example just given would be burdened with a huge tax bill, because most of the $140,000 loss reserve in this example might not be deductible under the current interpretation of the rules. Only insurance companies can deduct loss liabilities that are not clearly established and quantifiable.

This discussion of taxes and accounting all may be rendered hypothetical because the Exchange Board has chosen to withdraw its request for a ruling from the IRS. This move raises some thoughts that chances for a favorable ruling were not good.

How Lloyd's Keeps Books

Without a favorable IRS ruling, U.S. syndicates might opt for a method of reporting similar to that of Lloyds, which the IRS accepts. Lloyd's bookkeeping in effect eliminates reserves. The syndicates keep their books for a given year. For example, 1975 accounts were not closed until year-end 1977. At that point, a syndicate manager has a better fix on what the losses were on 1975 policies. After determining the underwriting and investment profits and paying out a distribution, the syndicate in effect goes out of business.

Any potential losses that may be carried over, such as claims arising from the side effects of a new drug that show up many years later, are then reinsured by the new syndicate when it is formed the next year, or by another reinsurer. If the new U.S. syndicates opted for this system, they would still pass tax-exempt income as well as underwriting gains or losses through to investors, but they would not generate the losses produced by statutory accounting.

The final option for syndicates would be to incorporate, making them miniature insurance companies. They would then pay taxes like any other insurer and their dividends to shareholders would be fully taxable. John Cox, Executive Vice President, Insurance Company of North America and a Governor of the Exchange argues that even this kind of structure would have investor appeal. "Many investors avoid insurance stocks because the companies are saddled with a lot of heavily regulated business. The syndicates will give people a way to invest in an attractive part of the industry."[2]

Regulation by N.Y. Insurance Department

It has been said the New York Insurance Exchange will be a self regulating entity, as Lloyd's is. It is hoped the system will encourage self policing. However, the Exchange's Board of Governors reserves the right to audit Exchange members' books.

There is concern, however, about the intentions of the New York State Insurance Department. The department has restricted the

---

[2] *The Review,* "The Insurance Exchange trying to get off the ground," August 29, 1979, p. 54.

freedom and flexibility of New York insurers in the past. There is fear that the Department will try to exercise regulatory control over the New York Insurance Exchange, the very thing the new market was designed to avoid.

The Superintendent, Albert Lewis, has stated: "There will be no interference in the operations by the Department. The Exchange will be self governing, self operating and self policing . . . the Department's involvement as a regulator will be extremely small, hopefully none at all."[3] But bureaucrats earn their living by regulating the insurance industry. Mr. Lewis has confirmed that the idea of an unregulated part of the insurance industry has aroused fears among some of his staff that their jobs may decline in importance or disappear altogether.

Senator John Dunne, Chairman of the New York State Insurance Committee, has said publicly that he is nervous about Mr. Lewis, particularly because the insurance department had set aside $250,000 for a bureau whose sole responsibility is to regulate the Exchange. "When we tried to eliminate the $250,000 from the budget, he (Lewis) vigorously opposed it. I fear that creating a regulatory bureau for a supposedly non-regulated Exchange portends something other than what was originally envisaged . . . I am deeply troubled that this may be a signal as to what the policy of the department will be."[4]

Competition from Within the U.S.

Another view of the Exchange is that it is simply not needed. This view comes from Chuck McAlear, a principal of the excess/surplus lines brokerage firm bearing his name in Grand Rapids, Michigan. He says the Exchange will have competition from within the U.S. as well as from London. He says:

"The Exchange is becoming a reality at a time when a marketplace that has already accomplished its avowed purposes is firmly established and has already proven itself.

"Though spokesman for, against, or on the fence regarding the New York Insurance Exchange, have studiously avoided mentioning that there was any competition but London, this is not the case.

"For reinsurance, there are professional reinsurance companies

---

[3] *Institutional Investor* "Can the New York Exchange get off the ground," June 1979, p. 133.

[4] IBID, p. 134.

in this country and abroad as well as reinsurance departments of various carriers who accept business directly or from brokers. For direct placement there is a marketplace instantly available to every agent throughout the country no farther away than the nearest telephone, linked electronically, allowing immediate utilization of the combined capacities of underwriters across the country and abroad. Through this network, a risk can be presented to dozens of underwriters, quoted and bound while an agent or broker on a trading floor is queuing up to see if a single underwriter will assume five percent of the risk.

"Moreover, this is a market of firm quotes and instant binders not plagued by 'indications' which can prove to be only that or 'subject to completion.' Nor does the market close down for weeks at a time when a lead underwriter takes a vacation.

"It is a market where all the underwriters assuming risk disclose their financial and business capabilities with the quotation, so appropriate judgments can be made before a firm order is placed.

"It is a market legally operating in various states, that reports its activities to the appropriate commissions and which pays minimum taxes to the individual states. It is a market of no surprises where continued coverage does not depend on the economic well being of individual carriers beyond the reach of regulatory authorities.

"Yet, spokesmen on the subject of the Exchange speak only of London. They have not mentioned Boston or Chicago or Los Angeles. How could Denver, Scottsdale, Haddonfield or Evanston Harbor compete with a grand New York Insurance Exchange? Yet this is the real competition. It is a group of companies who choose to accept business on a surplus lines basis from a network of brokers already in a place, who can provide immediate access, for a large or small agent, to their capabilities.

"It is a market which is proven. While standard carriers cowered and London markets proposed forms to protect their underwriters more than the client, this market singlehandedly prevented the liability panic from becoming a rout."[5]

Exchange Legislated in Illinois

While the New York Insurance Exchange has started out slowly and has run into some problems, this is not to say it isn't a good

[5] *Business Insurance,* "Surplus Lines Team Rivals, The Promise of the New York Exchange," June 25, 1979, pgs. 36, 37.

idea. At least some seem to think so. Witness the efforts being made to set up exchanges in Illinois and in Florida.

The Illinois Exchange's fundamental difference from the New York Exchange is that there will be no restrictions, such as a Free Trade Zone. This has caused consternation in other states, who fear they may lose business to the Illinois Exchange. This could cause some political repercussions.

But optimism has been expressed for the Illinois Exchange because of the state's unregulated insurance atmosphere. Illinois has been called the excess and surplus lines capital of the United States.

Other differences between the Illinois and the New York Exchanges is that only $2,000,000 in capitalization is required, and a provision that nothing in the Illinois insurance code is applicable unless stated. In New York, the code is all applicable except where otherwise stated.

The Illinois Exchange opened for business in November, 1981, with three syndicates formed by insurers Crum & Forster, Sentry and Reliance.

Insurance Exchange of the Americas

A move is underway to set up an Exchange in Miami, Florida. The proponents' idea is to attract a large volume of business from Central and South America. While a $50,000 study by Robert Hughes Associates determined that a low volume of premiums was available, the Insurance Exchange of the Americas plans to officially open late in 1982.

Whether insurance exchanges will flourish in the United States is the subject of much speculation. With the many considerations involved, it simply may be difficult to convince people to switch from the dominant Lloyd's market to the U.S.

Also, U.S. companies are no longer restricted from participating in Lloyd's. Yet, with many of the financial centers of the world located in the United States, it might be advantageous to establish institutions comparable to Lloyd's. The U.S. certainly has the talent and initiative to do so. The use of Exchanges should be looked at by risk managers as an available alternative tool in risk management.

13

Brokers, Agents and Other Intermediaries

As much as 95 percent of all of the insurance, including surety coverage, purchased by a corporation is done through an insurance broker. Brokers are best described as intermediaries between the insurer and insured. Ostensibly they represent the interests of the insured. In reality, however, the interests of the insurer and the broker are in concert and somewhat dissonant with those of the insured. This makes for a complicated relationship, whose understanding is absolutely essential to any intelligent appreciation of corporate risk management.

How Brokerage Evolved

Let us attempt to examine this multifaceted element to corporate risk management called insurance brokerage. One can hold two theories of how our present insurance brokerage setup evolved. And these theories, incidentally, are not mutually exclusive, so the truth may well be some combination of both.

The first theory is that, by and large, the present insurance brokerage firms and hence the speciality, evolved from the casualty insurance agent. From its inception, the insurance agency system, independent from any substantial degree of control by any insurer, has been the sales arm of the fire and casualty insurance companies.

As the insurance agent's corporate customers grew in size and complexity, the need to actually sell the insurance protection diminished. According to this theory, the need for insurance protection became obvious to the corporate owner or manager and the greatest need became advice and counsel as to the best approach to take care of risks. As a consequence the insurer's sales agent evolved into an advisor or counsellor to the customer, i.e., the broker.

Certain residuals of the former relationship between insurer and sales agent now turned broker still exist. Most notably, the broker is still often compensated by the insurer, not by the insured being served and whose interests are being looked out for. The amount paid is still apt to be some percentage of the premium paid by the insured to the insurer.

The fact that many of the present insurance brokerage firms were once insurance agencies and that in some instances they still hold agency contracts lends credibility to this theory.

The other theory is simpler. It holds that, sometime after the turn of this century, the relationship between the insurer and the corporate insured became complicated enough that the need for a third party became evident, and that intelligent, resourceful persons stepped into this vacuum to help work out the proper relationships. The proponents of this theory point to a similar evolution in other fields, such as advertising and real estate.

Operations Today

How do those who practice in this area operate now and what function do they serve? Like all significant facets of the risk management speciality, there is considerable difference of opinion. Let us examine these differences and see if we can't arrive at a consensus.

There are risk managers who are ardent believers in the do-it-yourself-let's-not-get-involved-with-brokers concept of risk management. But even they would probably acknowledge that they need the assistance of a competent insurance broker to place a new, complicated risk with the conventional insurance market, especially if the risk is large enough that several insurers must be persuaded to take part of it.

This is a prime responsibility of the insurance broker—to be the expert on the existing insurance market, its availability, the prevailing prices being charged and other attributes of marketing.

At the other end of the scale is the risk manager who strives to run every detail of the corporate insurance program through the brokerage firm before a decision is made. If this pre-decision coordination is not possible, this risk manager then discusses the decision in detail with the broker as a double check.

Somewhere between these two extremes is found the majority of risk managers.

The Role of the Broker

The capable broker, like the capable risk manager, learns as much about the operation of the corporate insured as is humanly possible.

In this way the significant perils to which the corporation is subject are determined and, where possible, systematically ameliorated. Many brokers have within their own shops sufficient underwriting capacity to supplement those of the insurer in determining the optimum treatment for the risk.

The broker employs engineers to study and determine proper loss prevention equipment to be installed, appropriate periodic inspection routine, follow up, etc. The broker's loss adjustment department will assist in the settlement of all insured losses suffered by the corporate insured.

In addition, the broker often maintains underwriting data of a fairly detailed nature which relieves the insurer of doing so. Probably the most important quality the broker brings to this three-party relationship is a detached view of the arrangements, the financial considerations, whether these be premiums paid to the insurer or losses reimbursed to the insured, and other considerations between the two primary parties to these transactions. Such detachment is not possible by either of the two primary parties, since both have heavy financial interests in these transactions, while the broker does not, or at least not nearly to the same extent.

The broker has still another function. It justifies, to a considerable extent, the approach of the risk manager who runs every detail past the broker either prospectively or on a double check basis. It is to serve as this double check. The reasoning to support this need is persuasive and goes something like this: First, the subject is complicated. Second, the insurance contract is uncertain. It becomes operable upon the occurrence of an event which is itself uncertain.

Finally, there is a great disparity between the dollar value of the premium paid and the value of the compensation received if the contract becomes operable. This disparity makes it especially important that all essential details of the contract be clearly understood by all parties concerned before the contract becomes operable.

Brokers *vis a vis* Self Insurance?

All the above described duties of the broker pertain to transactions and activities which take place when it has been decided to insure a risk. Can the broker participate in decisions which dictate self insuring the risk? And does the broker, practically speaking, so participate? The answer is "of course." The 1973–75 insurance capacity crunch changed the brokerage business too. The brokerage industry too, is "unbundling." The result is that the brokers are offering their service on a commission basis or on a fee basis.

Commissions are, of course, the payments to the broker by the insurer, computed as a percentage of the premium amount. Fees are the remuneration paid to the intermediary—a broker or a consultant—by the party receiving the service, in this instance the corporate insured. It is computed on the basis of time spent in doing the job or on some other measurement.

A Matter of Self Interest

The question of fee vs. commission was once considered germane to the larger question of whether the broker could effectively participate in studies on behalf of the corporate insured. It was felt that if a broker's analysis and study should indicate that self insurance is in order, the broker would be faced with recommending a course of action that would reduce its own remuneration. It was theorized that this would require a degree of self detachment, even heroism, not often found in any of us mortals. At the present time commissions, fees in lieu of commissions, fees without regard to commissions or some combination of any or all of these arrangements are used.

It is appropriate, however, to review briefly how the industry arrived at this condition. Because this breakthrough has, in turn, been followed by far reaching changes in the structure and functions of the brokerage area that affect not only the broker's relationships with corporate risk managers, but also with insurers and purveyors of ancillary services, such as loss adjusting firms, actuarial houses and the like.

Direct Writers

Until the 1940s, probably all of the corporate insurance sold, whether of an employee benefits nature or property, liability and other casualty coverages, were all sold through the insurance brokerage system, with three exceptions. These exceptions, all direct writers, were the Factory Mutual fire insurers, Liberty Mutual Insurance Company—a liability insurer with heavy emphasis on workers' compensation—and a few insurers, sometimes organized on a stockholder-owned basis, sometimes as a mutual insurer organized by certain industries with hard to place risks.

World War II and its aftermath changed the picture, beginning in the employee benefits area. During these years a significant number of employee benefit plans, in particular those negotiated as a result of collective bargaining agreements, were serviced by either brokers or consultants on a fee rather than a commission basis. What exactly influenced this change is hard to say. Perhaps it was because the life insurers predominated in this area rather than the fire and casualty insurers.

The life insurers developed an in-house sales force so, by and large, they were not as dependent on independent intermediaries (agents and brokers) as the fire and casualty insurers.

The tendency toward a consultant-fee arrangement and away from the broker-commission arrangement may also have arisen because of the influence of labor unions who often participated in the management of plans arising out of collective bargaining. Whatever the reason, the payment of a fee rather than a commission became eminently respectable in the employee benefits field.

During the same period there was a significant trend away from insuring these plans, at least on a 100 percent basis, to plans involving partial insurance and partial trust investment or to a 100 percent trust arrangement. It is hard to say which came first—the increased tendency to pay the intermediary (who could be a broker and often was) on a fee basis or the movement away from the 100 percent insured basis to a split funded basis or a 100 percent trust arrangement.

The Case of Casualty Insurers

No such rush toward the fee system asserted itself among the insurers dealing primarily in property, liability and other casualty coverages. Until the severe dislocations arising from the 1973–75 capacity crunch and the subsequent glut, there appeared to be little appetite on the part of brokers and no appetite at all on the part of insurers to go the fee route.

The reasons are complicated. Rate filings by the insurers with the appropriate state supervisory authorities from time immemorial had contained an element for acquisition costs. This element had to be paid out to an intermediary and without discrimination. The direct writers and those who have surfaced since had no such element in their rate filings. Could these agency companies have made additional filings with this element of acquisition cost removed, thus permitting the coverage to be offered to the insured at a lesser cost? This lesser cost would be offset, in part at least, by the fee to be paid to the broker-intermediary by the corporate insured.

Of course the answer is yes, as far as the legal aspect is concerned, since the direct writers had done so for years.

'Unbundling' Takes Hold

The decrease in insurance capacity in the period from 1973 to 1975 caused risk managers and the brokers providing them service to seek solutions other than placing risks with insurers; insurers were insuring fewer corporate risks. This was particularly true for risks which insurers deemed had high potential for loss, or inadequate premium rates, or both. So self insurance programs were introduced in many corporate risk management programs.

Of course, the captive insurance concept took giant steps forward during this period. Excess insurance coverages positioned over greater self insurance programs, were also utilized much more frequently. Many of these innovative programs were introduced by insurers smaller than those who were reducing their writings.

When the larger insurers regained their equilibrium and their insurance capacity, the newer programs continued to become a larger factor in the insurance market. Thus, a crunch quickly turned to glut. I believe it accurate to say that the typical risk manager gained a substantial amount of control over the corporate insurance program at this time, since other means were now available to take care of corporate risk.

The effect of this new trend on the insurance broker was also dramatic. During the capacity crunch, the insurance broker still had to develop a program for the corporation it served. Typically, the broker had to develop a program with a specialty insurer, without substantial loss adjusting services to offer. The broker would then go to the excess and surplus lines insurance market to contract for the excess coverage required, ascertain whether an independent loss adjusting facility should be used for appropriate loss and safety services, and other aspects of the program to make it complete.

Thus began the unbundling of the insuring process and those ancillary services which had formerly been more or less under the exclusive control of the large conventional insurers. The emergence of risk management services departments in several insurers dealing in large corporate risk and most of the large insurance brokerage firms, attests to this.

Consultants Bring Objectivity

This brings us to the third category of intermediary, the consultant. Since consultants do not sell or broker insurance, they can be completely objective in their analyses for corporate risk managers. As a result, they recommend insurance or self insurance without fear of being influenced in their judgments by their own personal interests.

Independent consultants surfaced in the employee benefits area during World War II and its aftermath when, incidentally, the whole area of employee benefits exploded into prominence in the U.S. business world, both in cost and significance. This emphasis, in turn, was spurred by two significant developments. The first was the freeze on take-home salary and wages imposed by the federal government early in the war and the consequent emphasis on granting increases in the form of deferred compensation.

The company pension plan offered the most desirable qualities for deferral. Obviously, money being credited to an employee's pension account and not given as take-home pay could not be used by the employee to buy consumer goods, thus relieving the upward price pressure on scarce consumer goods. To this extent, at least, the emphasis placed on employee benefits rather than take-home pay reduced inflationary pressures.

There are some who disagree that this approach did reduce inflationary pressures. They claim the cost of funding these deferred employee benefits as a current business expense led to increased product prices. Further, these dissenters point out, these deferred benefits created huge amounts of funds seeking an investment outlet, in turn contributing to lower interest rates, and to inflation.

Benefits Become Negotiable

The emphasis on deferred employee benefits was coupled with another powerful element that dramatically changed the course of employee benefits, for they (whether of a deferred nature or not) were deemed negotiable items of compensation under the National Labor Relations Act in a manner identical to wages paid, hours of work, paid holidays and similar items. Labor unions began bargaining in earnest with the corporate employer in this insured fringe benefit area. At the time the company employee benefits program generally consisted of group life insurance coverage providing a death benefit of one year's pay, an accident and sickness plan providing a benefit of $25 to $50 a week for a maximum of six months if disabled by sickness or a non-work-connected disability and, in some cases, a limited pension plan. The company sponsored group medical plan, if it existed at all, consisted of a schedule type plan, meaning that the plan would pay a predetermined amount, as recorded on the schedule, for any surgery performed on the employee or a member of the employee's family and a per diem payment to help take care of the hospital bill for relatively short hospital stays—generally no more than 30 days.

Who Contributes How Much?

There was no standard proportion of the cost contributed by employer and employee. In the specific program described above the employer bore 50 percent of the cost of group life insurance and two-thirds of the accident and sickness coverage for income lost due to illness or non-work connected disability. The employer's contribution to the pension was about three-eighths of the total cost. The employer's contribution to the hospital-surgical insurance plan amounted to something less than one-half of the total cost.

Benefits Moved to Industrial Relations

The introduction of collective bargaining brought a profound change. The employee benefits program ceased to be an adjunct of the corporate insurance program and the exclusive responsibility of the finance department, of which the insurance or risk management division was a part. The personnel or industrial relations department, responsible for negotiating collective bargaining agreements, assumed substantial responsibility in this area.

Invariably the primary responsibility for the kind and amount of employee benefits, whether insured or not, became that of the personnel or industrial relations department. The risk manager assumed a somewhat secondary responsibility, in some instances, to administer the plans once they had been negotiated or otherwise settled upon and, in other instances, to negotiate the insurance contracts by which the insured employee benefits were provided.

During this period of substantial change within the corporate environment, there was an equally significant change in the conventional insurance market serving this area of corporate activity. More and more employee benefits were provided through trusteed plans than through an insurance arrangement.

The Consultant in Employee Benefits

The employee benefits consultant, paid on a fee basis, began to supplant the broker paid on a commission basis. Sometimes these consulting organizations were divisions of an insurance brokerage firm. More often, they were independent operations with a heavy emphasis on actuarial skills. It is interesting to observe that most of these consultants, even the most fee-oriented of them, usually had an insurance broker's license in their back pocket, and for good reason.

Virtually every corporate employee benefit program of any size had some aspect of insurance coverage in it. The consultant retained to analyze the program would do so and be paid on a fee basis. If the change arising out of this analysis resulted in the purchase of increased insurance coverages, it would often generate a commission mandated by the insurer's rate filings, the insurer's concept of what it had to do to be non-discriminatory. The back pocket broker's license would then permit the consultant to accept the commission. By this device the corporate insured's interest was best served.

Since the consultant has done virtually all the work in the way of plan design, evaluation, and similar features, it would seem that the corporate insured's interests are not particularly well served by having this commission go to a broker who had no opportunity to do any work to justify the payment of this commission. Remember that the insured had already paid the consultant's fee. The logic behind this is well nigh irrefutable. The consultant receiving the commission is thereby enabled to provide still additional service to the corporate insured.

The Consultant in Property-Liability

There are also insurance consultants who specialize in the property-liability area. If there is one coverage in this area which consultants tend to emphasize over others, it is workers' compensation, probably because there is a much greater incidence of self insurance in this coverage. There are, in fact, a number of consultants who specialize in self insured workers' compensation programs, providing inspection, engineering and similar services. Without exception, as far as I know, these consultants do not act as brokers, nor do they have a broker's license, even in their back pocket. That fact, and their claim of greater objectivity, make up the main thrust of their customer promotional effort.

Views on the Captive Broker

With all the complicating and sometimes conflicting features of these broker-consultant intermediaries, it is not surprising that the idea of establishing a captive broker has come up. Anyone contemplating such an arrangement should not underestimate the legal and practical problems inherent in it. Typical of this is the New York statute which prohibits more than a 10 percent contribution of the business of an insurance brokerage firm if it is directly or indirectly controlled by the source of the business.[1]

Even if this 10 percent rule were not in effect, there are other statutory and administrative limitations which could cause considerable difficulty. These include prohibitions against discrimination among corporate insureds and insurance brokers, illegal kick-backs and the like. We wonder if a captive insurance brokerage firm, no matter how rigorously the laws and administrative determinations are observed, could operate without extending at least some preference to the owner-insured.

A final word on the captive brokerage concept involves the attitude of insurers: they regard independent brokerage firms as a significant part of their sales effort.

I know of one arrangement which has been cited as an excellent example of a captive broker, but which is not that at all. I'll describe it in some detail since I believe it can be one way to solve some of the problems of the present relationship between corporate insureds and insurance brokerage firms, the most serious problem being the duplication of clerical and administrative efforts.

The 110% Solution

A dear friend of mine, now deceased, who spent practically his entire adult life working in the corporate risk management field, used to describe this as the problem with the 110 percent solution. He observed that the insurance broker and the insurance department of a customer were on a collision course. There was so much duplication of effort between the two that either one could add 10 percent to its cost and be able to do all the work done by both.

An insurance brokerage firm often mentioned as a good example of a successful captive brokerage firm is actually no such thing. It might possibly be described as an exclusive brokerage firm, as it acts in the place of a corporate insurance department. The brokerage firm is not, however, owned by the corporation; therefore, it is not a captive.

---

[1] Section 119 of the New York Insurance Law, Sub-Division 4a,b,c (See excerpts at end of chapter).

Using Excess Capacity

It is interesting to note how this exclusive arrangement came to pass. This brokerage firm operated until the early 1930s in a manner similar to hundreds of other firms of similar size. It had only two large corporate customers. It subsequently lost one account. This loss left considerable excess capacity in the brokerage firm. Happily for both the brokerage firm and its remaining client, this excess capacity was put to work doing much of the work which normally would have been done in the corporation's insurance department. This arrangement had its defects but it also represented an ingenious, intelligent approach. Could it serve as a prototype for things to come?

It's also happened in another industry. To reduce expenses, the metal container companies offer to set up can forming lines in the plants of their customers. The can companies call these "satellite" operations. Could a similar satellite plan be applied to the relationship between insurance broker and corporate insured and thereby minimize the duplication of effort? I'm not talking about a physical amalgamation of the two, but a division of effort as logical and as intelligent as the arrangement between the can companies and their customers to reduce expenses. Such an arrangement would benefit both parties.

Lessons from Lloyd's

An interesting aspect of insurance brokerage is its dealings with Lloyd's of London. The syndicates, which are the real risk bearers in Lloyd's, get along with very few employees. Syndicates' books of account and other necessary records are maintained by the central management office of Lloyd's. The personnel of the typical Lloyd's syndicate is composed primarily of principals (partners) and underwriters. Both groups seem to devote their time to evaluating the risks being offered through the migration of the underwriting "slips." Perhaps it is partly because of this paucity of personnel, that the Lloyd's syndicates deal only with Lloyd's brokers.

Dealing Direct with Mutual Companies

A small percentage of corporate risk is placed with direct writing insurers. It is no coincidence that most of these direct writing insurers are organized on a mutual basis. At one time the overwhelming number of mutual insurers engaged in writing property, liability and other casualty lines were direct writers. It was their hallmark. The dividends to policyholders represented a share of the savings in operations arising from the fact that the mutuals didn't pay these monies out in acquisition costs.

In recent decades, however, many of the mutuals have seen fit to pay brokers a commission on the business they place with them. Again the conclusion seems inescapable that the broker is still the sales arm of the insurer, whatever relationship may have developed with the corporate insured.

Excerpts From Section 119 of the N.Y. Insurance Law

The superintendent may refuse to issue a license or renewal license, as the case may be, to any applicant if he finds that such applicant has been or will be, as aforesaid, receiving any benefit or advantage in violation of section one hundred eighty-eight, or if he finds that more than ten percent of the aggregate net commission, received during the term of the existing license, if any, or to be received during the term of the license applied for, by the applicant, resulted or will result from insurance on the property and risks:

(a) of the spouse of an individual applicant; and of any corporation of which such individual applicant or his or her spouse or both own more than fifty percent of the stock; and of any affiliated or subsidiary corporations of such corporation, and of the members of any firm or association and their spouses, of which firm or association the individual applicant or his or her spouse is a member.

(b) of the members of a firm or association applicant and their respective spouses, and of the owners of any interest in such firm or association and their respective spouses, and of any corporation of which such firm or association or the members or owners and their respective spouses, either individually or in the aggregate, own more than fifty percent of the stock, and of any affiliated or subsidiary corporation of such corporation, and of any other firm and the members thereof and their respective spouses, of which other firm a member or members of the firm or association applicant and their respective spouses are members or owners.

(c) of the stockholders of a corporation applicant and their respective spouses, and of any affiliated and subsidiary corporations of such corporation applicant, and of any subsidiary and affiliated corporations of a corporation owning any interest in such corporation applicant, and of any firm or association and the members thereof and their respective spouses which either individually or collectively own more than fifty percent of the stock of the applicant corporation, and of any corporation of which such firm or association and its members and their respective spouses, either individually or in the aggregate, own more than fifty percent of the stock, and of any affiliated or subsidiary corporation of such corporation.

Nothing contained herein shall be deemed to disqualify any applicant by reason of acts done or facts existing at a time when the same did not, under the law then in force, constitute nor contribute to constituting such a disqualification.

14

Financial Decision Making

Any specialty or profession has its problems and risk management is no exception. We present the following problems in risk management in the hope that abstract theory may be clarified through concrete application.

As with all problems that require making assumptions, someone else might arrive at different answers from the ones given here. The important thing is to state the solution used, so the assumptions made can be validated or modified, based on experience.

The Proper Deductible for a Fire Insurance Contract

Here is an actual problem faced by a company:

Should the deductible for its fire insurance contract be increased from $100,000 to $500,000? The higher deductible would reduce the premium by $40,000.

A quick calculation suggests that the $100,000 deductible should be retained. The maximum loss involved ($400,000) divided by the $40,000 annual savings gives the figure 10. Can the corporation go for 10 years without having a $400,000 loss in its 160 plant, office and warehouse locations with values in excess of $100,000? It is difficult to envision.

If we stopped the calculation at this point, there would be no justification for raising the deductible to $500,000 and the consequent increase in self insured exposure. But let us see what we find by a more systematic approach, using every known fact pertinent to a successful evaluation.

First let us ask a pragmatic question. If the insurer can see fit to accept the risk of loss for the suggested premium, why can't the corporation?

The corporation has a thing or two going for it that the insurer does not. The insurer has to pay a state tax ranging from two to four percent of the premium. In most states the corporation would not. More often than not the insurer has to pay an acquisition cost out of the premium ranging from five to twenty percent.

These two costs, plus the additional costs inherent in introducing a second corporate entity—the insurer—into the picture, suggest that, if the insurer has priced the risk with accuracy, it has to be more economical for the corporation to self insure the risk.

Let's try a more exact calculation to see how long it would take to accumulate a fund which could be used to pay the maximum amount of the loss if it should occur. And let's not ignore the fact that the fund can earn income—interest or dividends—fully as much as if it were in the hands of the insurer.

Accumulating a Self Insurance Fund

Let's assume the self insurance fund can earn five percent income after tax, which is not too difficult in these days of high interest rates. Such a calculation is included in Table I. This table illustrates several important points of risk analysis for purposes of developing the optimum amount of risk to be self insured. Note that the time interval needed to accumulate the amount necessary to take care of the loss is not 40 years or even 20 years.

TABLE I

	Annual Addition to Fund	Federal Tax Liability (at 50%)	Annual Addition (Less Tax)	Interest Earned (at 5%)	Total Amount in Fund
1st yr.	$ 20,000	$ 10,000	$ 10,000	—	$ 10,000
2nd yr.	20,000	10,000	10,000	500	20,500
3rd yr.	20,000	10,000	10,000	1,025	31,525
4th yr.	20,000	10,000	10,000	1,575	43,100
5th yr.	20,000	10,000	10,000	2,100	55,200
6th yr.	20,000	10,000	10,000	2,700	67,900
7th yr.	20,000	10,000	10,000	3,350	81,250
8th yr.	20,000	10,000	10,000	4,000	95,250
9th yr.	20,000	10,000	10,000	4,700	109,950
10th yr.	20,000	10,000	10,000	5,450	125,400
11th yr.	20,000	10,000	10,000	6,200	141,600
12th yr.	20,000	10,000	10,000	7,200	158,800
13th yr.	20,000	10,000	10,000	8,100	176,900
14th yr.	20,000	10,000	10,000	9,000	195,900
15th yr.	20,000	10,000	10,000	8,800	215,700
	$300,000	$150,000	$150,000	$65,700	

The table stopped when $200,000 was reached and not at $400,000, the gross amount of the loss. This is because the loss, if it occurs, generates a federal tax credit. It is only logical that, if the additions to the fund are calculated on an after-tax basis, so should the loss charged to the fund.

Another striking feature of this calculation is that it illustrates how prominent a role the interest factor plays in taking care of risk. Note that, during the 15-year term needed to fund the maximum loss, the interest grows to where it practically equals the annual addition after taxes.

Continuing this chart to the 23rd year, as has been done in Table II, illustrates another striking feature. Note that, while it took 15 years to accumulate enough in the fund to take care of the maximum possible loss, it takes only half as long to attain that amount again, assuming of course, that no losses have been paid out of the fund.

TABLE II

	Annual Addition to Fund	Federal Tax Liability (at 50%)	Annual Addition (Less Tax)	Interest Earned (at 5%)	Total Amount in Fund
at end of					
15th yr.	$300,000	$150,000	$150,000	$ 65,700	$215,700
16th yr.	20,000	10,000	10,000	10,800	236,500
17th yr.	20,000	10,000	10,000	11,800	258,300
18th yr.	20,000	10,000	10,000	12,900	281,200
19th yr.	20,000	10,000	10,000	14,000	305,200
20th yr.	20,000	10,000	10,000	15,000	330,400
21st yr.	20,000	10,000	10,000	16,500	356,900
22nd yr.	20,000	10,000	10,000	17,800	384,700
23rd yr.	20,000	10,000	10,000	19,200	413,900
	$460,000	$230,000	$230,000	$183,900	

Time Value of Money

The dynamics of the interest factor—or time value of money—looms most importantly in the handling of risk. Insurers are well aware of this. Risk managers are becoming equally alert to it. One risk manager I know persuaded his company to self insure as much of all insurable risks as it can without financial embarrassment, rather than insure these risks. He would still elect to self insure the risk we are discussing here even if he was fairly certain that a substantial loss would occur within the 14-year period necessary to fund the maximum loss.

This risk manager justifies his position on the basis of what he calls, somewhat humorously, the ex post facto loss theory—you are correct, he's a lawyer by training! He reasons that, except for the very large, truly catastrophic losses, the insurer expects to receive enough premium from a company of any size to pay for losses plus the expense of servicing these losses. If a loss occurs, the renewal premium is increased to reflect the fact that the insurer paid that loss.

Accordingly, if the company does have a loss which exhausts the self insurance reserve, this use of the reserve stops the ex post facto premium increase. In the interim, according to this risk manager, the company has the use of the monies not paid to the insurer. As indicated by the tables this can provide sizeable interest returns.

No Alternative to Insurance—At Times

Getting back to the original problem of how large a deductible, a casualty actuary could be retained, if necessary. The actuary could develop probability tables to help the company evaluate the risk. Accepting the percentage of probability developed by the actuary is not foolproof, of course. If it is important that the company not have an uninsured loss at all—such as when it has a covenant in a bond indenture that its properties must be insured—the company has no alternative but to insure this risk.

Sometimes a cooperative insurer can be found who will insure the reserve. That is, an insurer will agree to indemnify the corporation for losses in excess of the reserve.

How to Expand Risk Absorption

Some years ago Richard E. Stewart, then New York State Insurance Superintendent, delivered a speech entitled "Ritual and Reality in Insurance Regulation," in which he articulated four areas of insurance in need of attention. These areas were (1) the need for easier access to auto insurance; (2) protection against (policy) cancellation; (3) security in case of insurance company insolvency, and (4) open competition in rating.

In addition to identifying the problems then facing the insurance industry, it contained some philosophy which is worth repeating. Take for instance the following:

"For any institution, the alternative to intelligent change is not permanence; it is extinction.

"For any industry regulated in the public interest, the alternative to regulation is not freedom; it is replacement.

"To recognize the need for change and to welcome it, is a sign of strength, not of weakness. An institution that can justify evolution only by invoking the spectre of imminent disaster is likely to be an institution incapable of renewing itself from within. Better that we plan our changes calmly and without waiting for crises."

These comments, which are certainly pertinent to the specialized subject we're going to discuss, namely, insurance capacity, appear to be pertinent to the whole spectrum of property-liability insurance.

Capacity Defined

Perhaps it would be wise to define capacity. One insurance dictionary defines it as "the measure of an insurer's ability to issue contracts of insurance." It gives as a secondary definition, "the maximum volume of business which the company is prepared to accept."

I know of no scientific formula by which capacity is calculated, but there are many rules, guidelines and rules-of-thumb by which capacity is determined, or at least estimated. The rule which comes first to mind is that of the New York State Insurance Department which stipulates that no insurer can write a policy of insurance for more than one-tenth of its surplus. Thus, an insurer that has a surplus of $5 million would be limited to issuing an insurance policy calling for indemnification of a loss of $500,000.

The effectiveness of this yardstick is somewhat obliterated by the fact that that portion of a risk taken by reinsurers recognized by the state is not considered in making this "ten times" calculation. And, as a practical measure, few if any insurers actually approach this maximum "ten times" ratio in their underwritings. Invariably the risk assumed is much less than the permitted maximum. One yardstick often used measures the insurer's capacity by comparing premium to surplus; if property insurance is involved, a ratio of two-to-one is considered acceptable, and a three-to-one ratio of premiums to assets if casualty insurance is involved.

In his speech, Mr. Stewart said, "The accepted loss ratios in much property and liability insurance indicate that people so value the ability to transfer certain risks that they will contribute a third to a half of their premium dollar to the operating expenses of the risk distribution system."

Industry and Private Funding

Let us enlarge on this thought to see how capacity might be provided through industry and private funding methods. To be practical, such industry or private coverage has to be accomplished more efficiently or less expensively than through the conventional insurance market.

Mr. Stewart was referring, of course, to the expense element in the premium dollar—that is, that part of the premium dollar used for purposes other than the payment of losses. Most of those dealing in insurance activities are accustomed to having this expense come to their attention as the unspoken complement of the loss ratio percentage.

Thus, the 65 percent loss ratio generally regarded as standard, or at least a starting point for analytical purposes in workers' compensation coverage, leaves the expense ratio at 35 percent. For auto liability, a loss ratio of 60 percent is often regarded as standard; so the expense ratio is 40 percent. In fidelity coverages, these ratios are 50–50. In fire insurance, there probably isn't much unanimity as to what the loss-expense break point is. But a split of 40 percent loss to 60 percent expense would be most often mentioned by specialists in fire insurance.

Discussion of these loss ratios can be surprising, even disturbing, when presented by people who wish to reform the insurance industry. Who has not been disturbed when Messrs. Keeton and O'Connell observe that, in auto insurance, it takes $2.20 to get $1.00 back to the insured—the people—whom the system is designed to benefit?[1]

Extraneous Costs

To arrive at this $2.20 figure, Professor Alfred F. Conard of University of Michigan Law School, who developed the comparison later adopted by Keeton and O'Connell, included such extraneous costs as fees paid to the plaintiffs' attorneys, court costs and judicial salaries. But auto insurance still has a 40 percent expense ratio.

A cost accountant analyzing these loss-expense comparisons would probably assume that the expense element is analogous to overhead in a direct labor plan overhead problem, while the loss figure is analogous to the direct labor element. Applying this cost accounting comparison would require simply dividing the expense element by the loss element. The same standard loss and expense ratios mentioned earlier would be used. Thus, in auto liability insurance, by dividing the 40 percent expense figure by the 60 percent loss figure determines that, for every dollar of loss paid on one's behalf, it costs 67 cents to get each dollar of that loss paid and provide those other services one expects from an auto insurer.

Let's take workers' compensation insurance and again apply the

[1] *Basic Protection for the Traffic Victim*, Robert E. Keeton and Jeffrey O'Connell, Little, Brown and Company, 1968.

customary loss ratios. (Of course, many companies may experience loss ratios different from the customary ones.) The expense element, based on the 65 percent ratio for workers' compensation, is 54 cents. That is, 54 cents are paid in expenses for each dollar of loss.

With fidelity insurance, the customary 50–50 ratio of loss to expense means that the overhead factor is 100 percent. One dollar is spent on expenses for every dollar of loss.

If we accept the 40 percent loss ratio for fire insurance, it means that there is $1.50 in expenses for every dollar of loss.

Are there any areas in the corporate insurance picture where this approach can be successfully introduced, thus providing capacity through industry and private funding methods and, by doing so, incidentally reducing the ultimate cost to the corporation of taking care of the risks? Let us review the methods which have already been tried, along with their related problems, and explore where these plans could be strengthened.

Before doing so, let's discuss briefly what most insurance practitioners perceive to be a temporary condition in the market, namely, the insurance industry capacity glut which asserted itself in the late 1970s and continued into the 1980s and has altered substantially these traditional expense ratios. As capacity continued to increase and competition waxed more robust, insurers used every available means to "shave" the expense ratios to obtain or retain corporate customers. For the past 30 years until 1979, the insurance industry has experienced a series of three-year "scarce capacity-high prices-up" cycles followed by "much capacity-lower prices-down" cycles. These three-year cycles were nothing short of amazing in their precision and consistency—until 1979 when the expected "up" cycle did not appear, and, at this writing the "down" cycle continues.

Because the traditional fully priced expense ratios as earlier described prevail for the most part in the up cycles, the do-it-yourself devices we are about to describe are much more attractive to the policyholder during up cycles. Despite the current capacity glut and continuing down cycle, a study of such devices may well be worthwhile; it has in the past.

The Intra-Industry Pool

The Aircraft Builder's Council was formed in the mid-1940s as a pool offering product liability protection to manufacturers of aircraft and aircraft components. The event which precipitated its formation is said to have been a ten-fold increase in premium costs—from 10 cents to $1.00 per $100 of sales. This, in turn, was precipitated by a year or two of severe losses by insurers. Once set up, the pool was a conduit providing several million dollars of insurance protection itself. It reinsured the upper levels of potential liability in the U.S. and London markets.

The council appeared to have two things going for it which, on the drawing boards at least, should have gone a long way to guarantee its success. The first was a high expense ratio for insurance coverage available in the conventional insurance market, giving the participants hope that they could see savings by this do-it-yourself approach. The second was the so-called indivisibility of many of the risks. This was best illustrated by one much publicized airplane accident in which it was alleged that the cause was a malfunctioning instrument which was made by one company, installed in a power plant made by another, while the power plant was, of course, installed in the airplane involving still another manufacturer. One could see how neat and orderly the defense of the inevitable products liability claim would be, if all three manufacturers involved were represented by one insurer and not by three insurers. This one insurer arrangement would certainly eliminate the possibility of one manufacturer bringing the others into the case and thus, in effect, "virtually making the case for the plaintiff" or, expressing the concept colloquially, "washing the industry's linen in public." If nothing else, this one insurer arrangement should have resulted in lower attorney's fees.

Paying for Others' Losses

Despite these two aspects going for it, the council has lost much participation of the industry it seeks to serve. To venture a guess why, one only has to examine the reasons given by one company which withdrew from the plan. As a reason for withdrawal, it indicated it felt that it was paying too much into the plan in proportion to its own losses. Put another way, the company felt it was paying for other companies' losses. No company likes to do that. Yet it does exactly that when it is fortunate enough to have its own losses running less than the expected loss ratio for the group as a whole.

Under an insured arrangement, this fact is not obvious. Under a pool arrangement it is obvious not only to the risk managers but, perhaps more significantly, to the executives to whom the risk managers report. Inevitably, the question is posed, "Why should we be paying our competitor's losses?" This suggests that any arrangement to share or distribute losses among a pool of participants will be more likely to succeed if each participant absorbs a substantial segment of its own loss or losses before a sharing of loss by the pool participants begins. In other words, the protection afforded by the pool should always be in excess of a substantial self insured deductible or retention. This assumption of loss should be high—high enough that, when the pool is finally called upon to pay a loss, the risk managers of the participants, together with members of top management to whom they report, can say of the member receiving the payment, "there, but for the grace of God, go I."

Effects of FASB No. 5

Even before the adoption of FASB No. 5, it was difficult for a corporation to develop a program in which it would absorb accidental losses, rather than rely on the customary transfer of losses to an insurance company. The striking exception was U.S. Steel. Big Steel was for years America's number one self insurer with a reserve on its corporate books to pay for losses as those losses appear. This company's annual report to stockholders would give a brief summary of its self insurance activity. Typical of this was one of its annual reports which showed that U.S. Steel maintained a $50 million reserve for insurance, another reserve for contingencies, which was over $40 million, and still another reserve of $9.4 million captioned "Accident & Hospital". The comments contained in the notes to the financial statement further explained these reserves as follows:

"U.S. Steel is, for the most part, a self insurer of its assets against fire, windstorm, marine and related losses. The insurance reserve of $50 million is held available for absorbing possible losses of this character, and is considered adequate for this purpose.

"The reserves for contingencies and accident and hospital expenses of $50.1 million, provided mainly in previous years by charges to operations, are held for exceptional unanticipated losses other than those covered by the insurance reserve."

During one year, under this self insured reserve program and typical of the pattern for all years of the period, U.S. Steel charged a total of $3.2 million to the insurance reserve. Presumably these were losses. This same amount was added to the reserve, thus restoring the total of $50 million. The reserve for contingencies was increased by $100,000. There were no charges. The accident and hospital reserve had charges of $25.6 million with an offsetting credit of the same amount.

It appears that, at this stage in the development of this company's self insurance program, the cost was confined to the actual losses sustained, that is, it was paying little or nothing comparable to the insurer's expense.

In building these reserves, the customary approach was to charge an appropriate amount as an operating expense and credit the same amount to the reserve. Losses during the period would reduce the reserve, but the unexpended balance of the reserve would be carried forward to the succeeding year in a manner identical to assets, liabilities and other balance sheet accounts.

Vertical Absorption

This procedure permitted a company to spread the impact of a major loss over several years of earnings and to systematically absorb a fairly severe loss without financial embarrassment. Let us call this treatment vertical absorption, as contrasted to horizontal absorption, in which a loss is spread over many homogeneous risks through the insuring process.

The vertical absorption method of handling risks has never really been used by American industry as effectively as its possibilities appear to offer.

Clearly there is a loss level—call it the predictable loss level or expected level—where an insurer assumes that a company of significant size will in effect absorb the losses it incurs, so the insurer increases the renewal premium accordingly. Does it not make sense that the losses up to the predictable or expected level be taken care of on the books of the company itself, with consequent savings represented by the expense attributable to these losses?

Perhaps one reason this vertical absorption method was not used very much even before FASB No. 5 was the attitude of accountants and auditors. Additions to a self insurance reserve were not deductible on the corporate income tax return, whereas premiums paid to the insurers were. So the corporate accounting department had to make an adjustment in preparing the company's tax return. An item was added to the list of items that must be reconciled between the company's books and the company's tax return.

Accountants' Attitudes

It is difficult to explain why this adjustment loomed so importantly in the minds of accountants and auditors, often causing them to take a negative attitude to the self insured approach. There is logic, of course, in insisting that this adjustment not be made necessary for an inconsequential amount of savings to the corporation. But the attitude of the accountant went beyond this.

The procedure was looked upon as unsatisfactory accounting. Any balance in a self insurance reserve at the end of an accounting period was what the accountants call a surplus reserve. That is, it was really an appropriation of part of the company's surplus and not at all analogous to almost any other entry on the balance sheet, including the depreciation reserve.

We sense that the accountants disapproved because these surplus reserves were rare—not often found on a company's balance sheet.

Let us reexamine the data from the annual report of U.S. Steel. We can assume that the $50 million reserve was generated from the savings derived by not insuring. This was generally how self insurance reserves developed.

U.S. Steel had the use of this fund. Let us assume this use is worth 5 percent, or $3.5 million a year. The losses charged to this fund in what appears to be a typical year were $3.2 million. Thus the financial benefit derived from the use of the fund goes a long way in taking care of the company's applicable losses. How much more efficient can you get!

FASB No. 5 made all of this past history but the concept of do-it-yourself risk absorption has appeared in two different forms. One is the concept incorporated into the Risk Retention Act, passed by Congress in 1981, which contemplates the risk pooling of product liability exposures by corporations susceptible to the risk, with little or no recourse to the conventional insuring process. This concept, as articulated, is silent as to the federal tax treatment of the unpaid loss reserves involved in this process.

At this writing, there is a move underway, spearheaded by risk managers, to introduce federal legislation to amend the current law and allow corporations a tax deduction for self insured reserves covering incurred but not paid losses. Essentially the aim of the Loss Reserve Deduction Committee is to achieve a tax deferral, rather than a tax deduction, similar to the federal tax treatment accorded insurance company loss reserves.

The Spread Loss Concept

Until recently the use of the spread loss concept was confined to the field of reinsurance. We are grateful to John M. Haker, CPCU, then of the Northwestern National Insurance Group (now part of Armco Insurance Group) for permitting us to reproduce the following paper, in which he describes the possible application of this principle to corporate insurance.[2]

"A little while ago, Northwestern National ran an ad for workers' compensation insurance advertising our program as 'the next best thing to self insurance.' We received an irate letter from an agent in Ohio asking: 'Why are you advertising self insurance? Self insurance takes money out of the pocket of the insurance company and agent. We should be fighting self insurance, not advertising that it is a good thing.

"We were not advertising self insurance but we *were* recognizing the importance and proper place of self insurance. As insurance people, we accept the basic rule that you assume the risks you can afford to assume, insure those risks you cannot afford to assume. After all, we practice this principle every day ourselves, for in a sense we are self insureds just as the industrial firm may be. We assume $50,000 net exposure on this line, $75,000 on that line and so forth, reinsuring above what we can afford to retain. We therefore have much in common with the risk manager.

Retention Levels

"The basic decisions as to the amount of risk we retain per loss and on an aggregate basis are made by the management of the insurance company, just as the management of an industrial firm must make the basic decisions as to how much of the corporate surplus to risk before purchasing insurance coverage. Top management makes these decisions but the risk manager must suggest the amount which he considers as the basic working layer of loss, the amount beyond that working layer which he feels that the corporation can reasonably assume, and just where the excess program should kick in.

"Someday you will accumulate your risks, including many considered today as business risks, and accept aggregate deductibles far larger than you do today. In the meantime, you devise self insurance programs on individual lines wherein you retain, usually on a per loss basis, as much as you reasonably can, without impairing corporate assets.

"Unfortunately, there is no guarantee that you will not hit an

---

[2] Address given by John M. Haker before Wisconsin Chapter of American Society of Insurance Management (now Risk and Insurance Management Society) on Nov. 20, 1969.

unusual frequency of loss within your retention, causing an abnormal drain on surplus. There is also no guarantee that this will not happen at a time when a downturn in the business cycle, a falling off of sales, or other factors such as strikes, may cause substantial business losses to the firm.

"The combination of abnormal risk costs and unusual business losses can cause management nightmares. Where management has nightmares, these nightmares have a way of being transferred to the risk manager. Factors such as these tend to reduce the retentions which a risk manager will recommend.

"Another concern is the matter of cash flow, particularly in property lines. Third party losses are often reserved far ahead of payment and the drain on cash is not so immediate. Property losses are paid right away and a high frequency in this area can cause severe restriction in available cash.

Setting Net Risk in Single Year

"There is no definite breaking point between retention and excess. Corporate management decides that the firm can afford to assume X dollars of pure net risk in a given year. If you set up a retention within which you self insure and that retention is on an excess of loss basis, it must be set at a level low enough so that an unusual frequency of loss within the retention will still not produce total loss dollars in excess of the guidelines set forth by corporate management.

"The risk manager in order to be sure he will not exceed management's guidelines, must set his per loss retention too low. This means the firm has to buy its excess cover starting at a level which may be well down into the working layer of loss. This is costly, as the insurance company must be paid for the services performed in this layer. The firm could reasonably retain a larger line if only the results could be more predictable.

"What can the risk manager do about this? First of all, he can buy some type of stop loss on his retention. In effect, this is what you get when you buy a retro. The maximum serves as your stop loss. However, retro has disadvantages for the firm which feels it can handle its own losses or safety engineering better or cheaper than the insurance company or feels that it doesn't want to pay the retro basic to the insurance company, or feels that the cash flow of the corporation is better under a self insurance plan.

"As a second alternative, you can forget the per loss excess cover and seek coverage on a pure aggregate basis, but this somewhat defeats the purpose of self insurance. You are back to asking the insurance company to take on a part of the risk. Further, although such covers are available in workers' compensation, they are expensive and the market is limited and shrinking. The market for aggregate excess on lines other than compensation is extremely sparse.

Must Pay Own Way

"With any large corporation, insurance is a transfer of risk only temporarily. Within the working layer of loss, the large corporation, in the long run, must pay its own way. This is elementary and you recognize it in the acceptance of large retentions, either by deductibles, by retro or through self insurance. If you can assume the risk within your retention and the only concern you have is that the experience within that retention is too volatile, that there are too many peaks and valleys, that management needs more stable results, then there can be an alternate solution.

"Let us contemplate an insurance program wherein you agree to settle your own losses, maintain your own statistics. Is this an insurance program? It sounds more like self insurance. However, if there is a temporary transfer of risk, it really accomplishes all you need in the way of insurance within your retention area.

"The spread loss device has been used for years by insurance companies to solve an identical problem—the problem of instability in results. An insurance company cannot go to its stockholders with wildly fluctuating composite ratios. Under a spread loss plan, the insurance company agrees that, in the long run, it will pay the freight; it only looks to its reinsurer to cushion the blow, levelling off the peaks and the valleys of its experience. Call it a funding device if you wish, a guarantee that the reinsurance company will come up with funds in the bad years to trim down that peak in losses. The concept can work also for self insureds.

"If such a cover were made available to self insureds by insurance companies, the self insureds would smooth out the results within their retention and the insurance company would not assume risks which rightfully belong to the self insureds. The only risk assumed by the insurance company, in the long run, is a credit risk, a very nominal risk when dealing with major industrial firms.

"In addition to levelling out the experience within your retentions, such a program would enable you to increase your retentions. Faced with more predictable results you can well consider the acceptance of higher risk. Such a program can also replace aggregate plans.

Akin to a Prospective Rating Plan

"Look at it another way. Under a retrospective plan, your loss costs are borne by you in the year in which they are incurred. The spread loss plan would be akin to a prospective rating plan, whereby you agree to pay over the next five years for what happens this year. You also agree that if you have a particularly good year, you will not gain the benefit immediately, but instead will obtain slightly reduced risk cost over the next five years.

"What about the cost of such a program? If you agree that you can assume the risk in the long run rather than asking the insurance company to assume your risk, then an insurance company could provide the function of levelling your experience for you at a much lesser cost than if they take the risk on your behalf.

"When insurance companies purchase reinsurance from their reinsurance sources, the markup of the reinsurers is not 100 percent over loss costs, as is the case with primary insurers. It is closer to 25 percent over loss costs or less. The difference? No engineering, very little claims control required, less commission, reduced taxes, licenses and fees and, since the business comes in larger chunks, reduced percentages for underwriting costs. Since risks are reduced, supply and demand reduce the percentage of contingency and profit built into the pricing. The same factors apply to the spread loss concept for self insureds.

"One further advantage of the spread loss concept: you need not lose control over claims, engineering, legal handling or any other facet of your self insurance program.

"What type of insurance could fit into this concept? Workers' compensation? General liability? Automobile? Fire? Actually there is no reason why the principle could not be applied to any of these or a combination thereof.

The Ironclad Contract

"How would such coverage be issued? It would have to be in the form of an ironclad contract whereby the self insurer agrees that the risk remain his. The insurance company agrees to pay the losses on behalf of the self insured only temporarily, for levelling purposes. Is this asking too much of the self insurer? No! The self insured has the risk now *without* the benefit of loss levelling. He can afford to retain the loss. He only needs the benefit of a cushioning of the blow.

"To sum up: why not a spread loss reinsurance program for

self insurers? They have the identical problem as insurance companies.

"They have one further, very important problem. Suppose you decide to self insure the first $100,000 of automobile liability exposure. At the end of the first year of your self insurance program, you find you have a considerable number of large cases pending, with unpredictable cost to the firm.

"Prudent accounting practice would require that you should establish reserves on your books, equalling the estimated cost of these liability suits. If you do not do so, you are overstating your profits for the year and imposing a burden on future years for debts incurred in the current year. However, if you do set up such a liability on your books, this is a business expense for which you are not entitled to tax credit.

"Uncle Sam will not allow your loss reserves as a tax deduction until the losses are paid. Had you bought insurance, instead of self insuring, the insurance premium would have been entirely deductible. The use of a loss levelling plan will enable you to take credit for reserved cases. This can be of particular advantage in a year with high profit margins.

"Obviously we are not talking about a traditional form of insurance policy. In format, it would be much closer to a typical reinsurance agreement. That is, a continuous form of agreement, cancellable only at the end of a policy year, with the express provision that debts incurred under the contract would continue until all installments thereof were met. You would establish the pay-in rate on the basis of anticipated losses within the retention and be reimbursed for actual losses within the retention.

Repayment Over Five Years

"The difference between actual and anticipated losses would be spread out for repayment over five years. This form would closely resemble the spread loss reinsurance agreement between insurance companies and reinsurers.

"Another possibility is a form of policy, more traditional in nature—a policy covering the specific line of insurance and written for whatever limit of coverage is desired.

"For example, an automobile liability policy written for 100/300/100 limits. Then there would be a prospective rating agreement (not retrospective) applicable to that portion of the limit which the insured wishes to retain. The contract would be continuous with the rating procedure spelled out in the contract. The insured would agree to pay his own claims within the self rating area of the policy or, if preferred, he could purchase claim handling services as part of the contract.

"The basic difference between this policy and a traditional insurance policy would be the continuous rating procedure (probably a loss rating formula) and the agreement not to leave the insurance company in a loss position. Because of the payback provisions, the insurance company's markup on the self rating portion could be well below the usual charges, particularly if the insured elects to handle its own claims.

"Using a policy form of this nature is particularly advantageous in the case of a firm which needs to make filings with various regulatory bodies. A multistate trucking firm, for example, needs to certify that it carries the limits of coverage prescribed by various regulatory bodies. Through a policy such as this, it can have filings made on its behalf and still have many of the advantages of self insurance plans.

"To sum up: it is my belief that the spread loss concept, so important to insurance companies, can be made to work as well for the large industrial firm interested in self insuring."

The above comments were given over 12 years ago, yet there is a freshness about them that renders them well worth repeating. One possible problem to the concepts described could be the emerging attitude of the IRS that any insurance program in which the premium paid is in the nature of a "deposit," i.e., adjustable up or down by events occurring subsequent to the execution of the contract, is considered nondeductible for federal income tax purposes. But the IRS position is far from clear, so there is plenty of room for continued study and adaptation of these creative concepts.

How Much Liability Insurance?

A corporation's liability for negligence or other wrongful acts is unlimited. So it is exceedingly difficult to say how much liability insurance it should carry.

The risk of liability is unlike property risk where the maximum loss is the total value of the property, plus the cost of business interruption. There is no such way to measure the extent of injury or damage to third parties by the corporation's conduct.

One astute risk manager illustrates the point by this example: Even though the owner of the Empire State Building carried liability insurance to cover replacement of the building and its contents, what would happen if the corporation were held responsible for its destruction? It would be virtually impossible to destroy such a facility without damaging the surrounding buildings and facilities.

The risk manager then asks if it would be prudent to protect the corporation against the loss of facilities within a radius of one or two miles of the building.

The Limits of Capacity

From a practical point of view, there is a limited amount of insurance capacity to take care of the hypothetical risks envisioned in this example. Practically speaking, there is probably not more than $500 million of liability insurance coverage available to any corporation from the conventional insurance market.

Those few corporations who have been held responsible for catastrophic losses, understandably enough, do not provide much information on the subject. But there is enough information available to state that liability coverage of $500 million is sufficient to take care of the liability claims made so far against any corporation from a single accident or occurrence.

Some corporations that are vulnerable to extremely high liability claims have adopted a simple answer to the question of how much liability coverage to carry. Their answer is "all that is available from the insurance market."

At least one company that already has the maximum amount of such coverage has given its broker a standing instruction to procure any additional layers of excess liability insurance coverage that may become available from the conventional insurance market.

Prudent to Insure

There is one answer, but an unsatisfactory one. If there are possibilities that the corporation will have to respond to liability claims of huge amounts of money, obviously it is prudent to attempt to have this risk covered in the conventional insurance market. It should also excite some thoughtful study of the whole risk handling and insuring process.

What is gained when the insurer of an airline, for instance, has to pay several million dollars to victims or their families following an airplane accident when the facts reveal that there was really no negligence—no fault, if you will—on the part of anyone, including the airline? It's difficult of course to argue that victims of any tragedy should not receive all they can get to help assuage their misery. But I do believe students of risk management and insurance must bring to this study a proper perspective. Measured by what most other victims of accidents receive, the victims of airline accidents receive a windfall. This is a destructive trend and a type of thinking we must move aggressively to counteract.

Minimum Limits

So much for the corporate behemoths with their huge liability risks. What about the smaller corporation which cannot afford to purchase even the $500 million of available liability insurance and must settle for something less than the maximum. Let's start on the bottom end of the scale and suggest a minimum.

There now exists a personal liability coverage for high salaried persons generally referred to as executive excess. The minimum amount of coverage is $1 million and $5 million is available to most executives. To my mind this describes the absolute minimum for any business, whether incorporated or not. Somehow, juries seem less inhibited in assessing liability against business generally and corporations in particular, than they are in assessing liability against individuals. If this assumption is correct, prudence would dictate that this eventuality be anticipated in the corporate insurance program.

This leaves a very wide gap between $1 million and $500 million. It is in this band that virtually all corporate risk managers find themselves. Unfortunately, the great uncertainty of the extent of this risk makes it impossible to set any criteria for measurement, except the following one.

Our system of law has developed the prudent man rule. It says that an individual has an obligation to act as any prudent person with reasonable intelligence would in the same or similar circumstances. This rule means that the standard of conduct is set by all of those who find themselves in the situation in question.

A derivation of this prudent man rule would suggest that the prudent risk manager or company would have at least as much liability coverage as other companies of similar size engaged in the same activity. Admittedly, this is a nebulous rule, but following it could be highly beneficial to the risk manager and his company.

15

Self Insured Retentions, Deductibles and Other Loss Sensitive Plans

Today a corporation of any size will have some form of loss sensitive insurance plan. This means that the ultimate financial outlay of the corporation for protection against the risk of loss is determined to some extent by the losses which occur under the program. The contract can be written on a self insured retention basis, on a deductible basis or on a retrospectively rated basis.

For these three loss sensitive plans the amount of loss which the risk taken is expected to bear can be calculated on an occurrence basis or on an aggregate basis. It can vary widely in amount, and depends on what the risk taker is willing to absorb as a current expense.

Self Insured Retention

A self insured retention, or SIR, is a conscious acceptance of the risk of loss by the company (or person) without recourse to any type of insurance. If loss occurs, it is charged to current expense or, in increasingly fewer instances for reasons we shall outline further in this chapter, to a self insurance reserve maintained on the company's books.

The academicians prefer to call this risk retention. Risk managers and others seem to prefer the terms self assumption (if no self insurance reserve is maintained) and self insurance if a reserve is maintained.

A self insurance reserve is an accounting device. A loss is not charged to current expense but to the reserve set up on the books for this purpose. Since funds must be available to take care of the loss when payment must be made, this reserve procedure contemplates that there be systematic credits to the reserve in amounts similar to the premium payments to an insurer if the risk were insured.

The capacity crunch of 1973–75 put a strain on the terminology in this area. Out of it came a fairly widespread agreement that any type of retention should be called a self insured retention, whether or not a reserve was maintained.

Under an SIR plan the party susceptible to the risk is legally responsible for the payment of all claims within the SIR layer of the plan. Above the SIR layer there is always excess insurance which is often written by the same insurer that administers the claims falling within the SIR layer.

Least Complicated, Least Expensive

Conceptually, this is the least complicated of the three loss sensitive methods, assuming there are no other considerations such as satisfying governmental requirements (as in workers' compensation insurance) or providing proof of insurance coverage (as in automobile liability in many states). What could be simpler, especially if no reserve is set up, than to ascertain the amount of the loss when it occurs and charge the appropriate amount to current expense?

The most compelling argument for a SIR plan is that this arrangement is often the least expensive. When the loss occurs, the party susceptible to the risk disposes of it without recourse to insurers or other parties who charge for their services.

Consider what occurs when the loss is insured. The loss is reported to the insurer, generally through a broker. The insurer has to satisfy itself that the loss did in fact occur and how much was lost. This could bring a fourth party into the picture, an independent loss adjuster, who investigates the loss and determines the amount of loss, whether or not the cause of loss brings it within the coverage of the insurance contract. Can more money be spent on adjusting the loss than the amount of loss itself?

Proponents of the full insurance concept argue that the insurer's loss administration must be consistent. By paying, without investigation, a small loss which should not have been paid under the terms of the insurance contract, the insurer would establish a precedent which could be used by the insured party to support a claim of reimbursement for a larger loss arising from the same cause. These proponents also argue that an insurer may not discriminate among its policyholders, a requirement imposed by statute and other insurance regulatory authorities. Obviously, inconsistency in loss reimbursement among insured parties could be construed as discrimination, illegal rebating, etc.

Thoughtful students of the subject accept these arguments as valid. But they also believe these are compelling reasons why an insured should elect not to insure those risks which it can itself absorb without financial embarrassment or at the sacrifice of some essential service obtainable only from the insurer. It seems obvious that the SIR approach, being so simple, should be the first one considered in analyzing the possible treatment to be accorded to any risk, especially for losses rather quickly ascertained and settled.

Deductible Plans

A deductible plan is the same as a SIR plan in all respects except one. The salient feature in a deductible plan not found in a SIR plan is that the insurer writing the deductible plan is a guarantor of payment for losses to third parties occurring within the deductible layer. No such guarantee exists in a SIR plan for losses occurring within the SIR layer.

Retrospectively Rated Plans

The retrospectively rated plan resembles a deductible plan with an aggregate feature. It is indistinguishable from other guaranteed cost plans except that the insurer adjusts the final premium retrospectively for losses over or under the normal loss level contemplated. A deductible plan does not include in the "going in" premium, provision for payment of deductible losses, so the plan provides that losses under the deductible be reimbursed to the insurer as those losses are paid by the insurer. Losses under a SIR are, of course, the legal obligation of the party susceptible to the risk and are paid as such. Under a retrospectively rated plan, the premium collected by the insurer is enough to enable the insurer to pay the losses on a current basis. The retrospectively rated settlement, as the name implies, is then accomplished sometime after the term of the policy ends.

Accounting and Tax Deductions

When losses under a SIR or a deductible plan are expensed on the company's books only when those losses are paid, no federal tax complication exists. All public accountants and the IRS will agree that the payment of such losses is an expense of operating the business and a valid deduction for income tax purposes. Difficulty arises only when losses are incurred but not paid.

The document which accountants operate under—Financial Accounting Standards Board, Standard No. 5, Accounting for Contingencies (FASB 5)—says that an unpaid loss may be charged as an expense on the books of the party susceptible to the loss, if (1) it occurred during the accounting period involved, and (2) the amount of the loss is reasonably determinable.

The first condition should pose no problem. The dates of losses from fires, windstorms and other forces causing physical damage to a company's assets are obvious. Liability or workers' compensation claims in most instances can be identified as to date of occurrence even in the difficult incurred but not reported (IBNR) aspect.

Difficulty arises in the second qualification—what constitutes a reasonable determination of the amount of the loss. Some public accountants (rather heavy handed in my opinion) equate a reasonable determination of the amount of the unpaid loss to a final offer of settlement. In other words, they seek to treat it the same as an unpaid rental item. Other public accountants are more liberal. They determine the amount of loss through the use of past loss experience, actuarial determinations and similar devices, and consider it an expense item for tax purposes.

Tax Treatment of Insurer and Self Insurer

To say that the present federal tax treatment of unpaid loss reserves under a self insurance program is chaotic is an understatement. Reportedly, the IRS districts vary from one extreme to another. On the one hand they may recognize these reserves in calculating the tax liability if it has been demonstrated that the occurrence giving rise to the reserve has, in fact, taken place and there has been a fairly professional (e.g., actuarial) determination of the amount of loss. At the other extreme, they may refuse to allow any deduction other than the paid loss.

It should be noted that when these same unpaid loss reserves show up on the books of an insurer, they are tax deductible. Why? If the IRS insists on seeing the cancelled check before permitting a tax deduction for the loss under a self insured program, why don't they insist on the same thing from an insurer? It's true that insurers are taxed under a different section of the tax code than self insurers, but both sections of the code speak in terms of reasonable and necessary expenses incurred in the business as deductions for tax purposes.

No one would question that a loss for which an insurer is legally obligated to pay, even though unpaid at the time of calculating the tax, is a reasonable and necessary expense of the insurer. Would any jury seriously hold that a food processor with 10,000 vehicles on the road incurring losses (property or liability) arising from accidents to those vehicles delivering its product to its customers, is not incurring reasonable and necessary expenses? Nowhere does the tax code require that the cost of these accidents be transferred to insurers to be tax deductible. Nowhere does the code give the specific right to tax deductibility to insurers or deny the specific right to the self insurer. Why then the anomaly?

Based on 10th Amendment

My theory is that the position of the Internal Revenue Service is based on the 10th Amendment to the U.S. Constitution, which says: "The powers not delegated to the United States by the Constitution, nor prohibited by it to the States, are reserved to the States respectively, or to the people." State laws and state insurance regulations permit, even require, insurers to consider their unpaid losses in calculating their earnings. Therefore, it has to be deemed a reasonable and necessary expense in running an insurance company, and hence deductible for tax purposes.

If this theory is correct, it might be appropriate for a lawyer more proficient in taxes than I am to examine these same substantive aspects in relation to self insurance. Self insurers, particularly those who self insure workers' compensation, operate under state statutory and administrative regulations, requiring the self insurer to conform explicitly to obligatory features of the coverage in a manner identical to an insurer. Would this not be enough for most juries to determine as fact that the self insurer was also entitled to the tax deduction?

16

The Captive Insurer

Captive insurance companies are devices set up to handle the insurance needs of business corporations. They may be owned by an industrial or commercial enterprise, an association of enterprises, a professional society or its members, or an association of local governments. These are organizations whose risks are not easily insured through the conventional insurance market.

Captive insurance companies can be based domestically or offshore. They can be property, marine, or casualty insurers or some combination thereof.

When several companies or groups get together to form a captive insurer, they are generally from the same industry and often suffering from a single exposure that is difficult to insure. A captive insurer also can be organized to insure U.S. or foreign risks, or both, of its parent or sponsor.

It could be argued that many mutual insurers, formed mostly in the mid-nineteenth century to provide insurance for specific industries, were at one time captive insurers. Most of them have since broadened their writings and are now part of the conventional insurance market.

A captive insurer can be organized as a stockholder-owned company, as a mutual, or as a reciprocal. At one time, the one common quality of all captive insurers was that their writings were confined to the risks of their corporate parents or sponsors and they did not hold themselves out to the public generally as accepters of risks. To do so would mean that, by definition, these insurers had ceased to be in the captive category and had joined the conventional insurance market.

Many captives still adhere to this policy of exclusive underwriting. Others, especially a captive of a single owner, have sought and written third party business (the first party being the owner and the second the captive) for reasons we shall explore later on in this chapter. These captives are motivated, at least in part, by Internal Revenue Ruling 77–316.

Less Expensive, More Efficient

A captive insurance company comes into existence because the owner or sponsor can thereby obtain less expensive or more efficient coverage, or both, than can be obtained from the conventional insurance market. The corporate decision to put a captive insurer on stream is essentially no different than countless other make or buy decisions being made constantly in American industry. These decisions range from whether or not it is economically sound to set up one's own electroplating shop or buy the service from the established industry; to buy or rent one's own computer or have the corporation's needs taken care of by outside companies; to form one's own in-house advertising agency, or rely on a conventional advertising agency to take care of the corporation's needs.

The corporate do-it-yourself proponent may be firmly convinced that the course of action will result in a better or less expensive arrangement. But the outside purveyors of the service will always believe that the do-it-yourselfers have erred somewhere in their assumptions and calculations. They will believe that the captive or in-house arrangement has not been costed properly, or is providing an inferior service, or suffers in some other way which can be remedied only by returning to the conventional purveyor of the service.

Insurance companies operate in vastly different ways than noninsurance corporations. For instance, the accounting rules and procedures for an insurer are significantly different than those employed by corporations generally. Insurers are taxed under a different section of the tax code. Because of these differences, it is a more complicated task to evaluate the economics of bringing a captive insurance company on stream than it is to evaluate the economics of forming an in-house advertising agency or deciding whether the corporation should do its own computer work or set up its own electroplating shop. Despite the complexity, a corporate risk manager should not fail to analyze thoroughly the economics of this arrangement.

Benefits of a Captive Insurer

The proponents of the captive insurance company concept would probably see as an advantage the fact that reserves established on the books of an insurer are deductible when computing federal income tax, while the comparable reserves for a self insurance program are not. This is a fact, but what monetary advantage does it give over a self insured arrangement?

The three types of reserves which provide favorable tax treatment for insurers are loss reserves, loss adjustment reserves, and unearned premium reserves.

Many types of reserves are found on the books of an insurance company, but all fall into two broad, significantly different categories. They are surplus reserves and profit and loss reserves. Surplus reserves are actually part of the company's surplus, such as reserves for investment fluctuations or the reserve some insurers with huge unrealized capital gains in their securities have set up for the federal tax liability applicable to such gains. Surplus reserves are never deductible in calculating insurance companies' federal tax liability. But profit and loss reserves are always deductible.Loss reserves, loss adjustment reserves, and unearned premium reserves, representing amounts the insurer expects to pay sometime in the future for these items, fall into this profit and loss category. These reserves provide a tax deferment and not a tax exemption. If any of the amounts placed in these accounts are not used for the purpose intended, tax becomes payable as a result of the reclassification of these items out of the reserve into underwriting profit.

Because all losses and loss adjustment expenses are tax deductible when actually paid out, the deductibility of such reserves is a tax deferral rather than a tax exemption. The difference between tax deferral and tax exemption is important. In effect a tax exemption provides a benefit of the full rate of taxation (probably about 50 percent), while a tax deferral offers an opportunity to earn money on the funds during the period of tax deferral. This tax deferral advantage can be considerable or nominal, depending on the length of time one has the use of the funds, the rate of interest that one receives, and similar considerations.

Tax Considerations

If the captive insurer is organized domestically (within a U.S. jurisdiction), one has to be especially careful in calculating the tax advantages. Although the corporate parent can take a tax deduction on premiums paid to the captive, it is important to consider what happens on the books of the captive insurer. To illustrate, let us assume the corporate parent pays $500,000 in premium to its captive insurer. Let us further assume that, at the end of the year, the books of the captive insurer show that $250,000 has been paid out in losses and $150,000 is resting in the three profit and loss reserves described earlier, leaving $100,000 as an underwriting profit on the books of the captive insurer.

The $250,000 of paid losses can be deducted in computing the insurer's federal tax, but this would also be true in a self insurance program. The $100,000 underwriting profit is subject to the same amount of federal tax as if that $100,000 had stayed on the books of the corporate parent. In fact, if the corporate parent and captive insurer file consolidated tax returns, which is the most sensible arrangement in most instances, the rules of consolidation require that all monies paid between the two corporations must be used to offset each other.

The result of this offset places the $100,000 underwriting profit in the same position as if it had stayed on the corporate parent's books. Clearly this profit factor—the amount over and above what the captive insurer needs to pay losses and expenses and what it can set up in profit and loss reserves—makes no contribution to diminution of federal taxes.

The $150,000 resting in the three profit and loss reserves is not subject to tax as long as the amounts are not excessive and are reasonable in relation to the amounts that will actually be paid out at a later date. The amounts carried in these profit and loss reserves would not be tax deductible in a self insurance program. This then is the principal tax advantage of the captive insurer arrangement over a self insurance program.

Loss and Loss Adjustment Reserves

To see how great this advantage is, let us analyze the loss reserves and the loss adjustment reserves together, since both are related. The loss reserves represent the amounts expected to be paid to the parties actually incurring the injury or damage, while the loss adjustment reserves represent the amounts expected to be paid to adjusters, investigators, lawyers, and similar personnel used to help determine and settle losses.

These reserves, which cannot be created out of thin air, are set up on a case-made basis. This means that, by and large, the insurance company has to have a case, or a claim, before it can initiate the accounting entry setting up the reserve. There is no denying that a considerable tax advantage arises to a casualty insurer who initiates a workers' compensation reserve approximately $300,000 for a 40-year-old claimant who will, actuarially speaking, be paid $200 a week for 30 years.

This example shows why workers' compensation coverage generates a large, deferred tax advantage. This is followed closely by liability coverages. The time that elapses between a fire or other property loss and the payment of such a claim is generally not as significant. Whatever the time element involved, this is the period in which the captive insurer has the use of the funds and earns income on the deferred tax.

Unearned Premium Reserves

There is less evidence that an unearned premium reserve provides a significant tax advantage to the domestic captive insurer. If the corporate parent and the captive insurer file a consolidated tax return, the premium paid from parent to insurer, must be used to offset itself. On the other hand, a premium would be completely deductible if paid to any other insurer.

The lack of deductibility can be partially overcome by permitting the captive to claim all of its costs and expenses paid out of the premium received from its corporate parent. This offsetting of the premium is logical and proper. To allow the corporate parent to deduct the premium, and the captive to deduct the losses and expenses, would result in duplicate deductions on the consolidated tax return.

Unfortunately, there are no costs or expenses attributable to this unearned premium which the captive insurer can claim to make up for the parent's loss of deductibility for the premium paid. As a consequence, the unearned premium reserve does not enjoy either tax exemption or tax deduction, if the tax returns of the corporate parent and captive insurer are consolidated for tax purposes. However, if separate tax returns are filed, the corporate parent uses the premium it has paid as a tax deduction, and the captive insurer can leave in its unearned premium reserve that part of its premium which it has not earned. This means that the premium is not considered taxable income until it has been earned.

Problems Raised by Separate Returns

This approach may raise a couple of problems. One is that the IRS may compel consolidation because the two companies are so closely related. The other is that, if the captive insurer should pay a dividend (from its own earnings of course) to its corporate parent, this transaction is taxed at the rate of about 7.5 percent. And it must be in the form of a dividend to stockholders, not a dividend to policyholders. If it were paid as a dividend to policyholders, it would have to be treated by the policyholder as a refund of insurance expense, which is taxable at the corporate rate of around 50 percent.

Offshore Captives

An offshore insurer is one formed and domiciled in a country other than the country in which the parent company is located. Bermuda and the Grand Cayman Islands are the most popular sites for captive offshore companies. Both are tax havens. Bermuda has achieved greater prominence, because it has been used longer for this purpose. Other locations such as Switzerland and the Channel Islands are sometimes used.

The most important attributes of a suitable offshore site are a low or nonexistent tax rate on the operations of the insurer, a banking system efficient enough to make rapid transfers of funds in and out of the country, a government with some stability, and a labor force sufficient to provide enough clerical, administrative, professional and managerial personnel.

Lack of Standardization

Until the mid-1950s, virtually the only available method of insuring overseas risks was to buy insurance in each country from the local insurers which, of course, comprised the country's conventional insurance market. A major difficulty was the lack of standardization among various countries as to which perils were being insured and to what extent.

For example, one western European country had a property insurance endorsement akin to the U.S. extended coverage endorsement. Indeed, the words describing it were often translated into the words "extended coverage." But this endorsement did not contain protection against loss from windstorm. When one U.S. risk manager inquired about this lack, the answer from the overseas subsidiary's management was that coverage was unnecessary, since no windstorms severe enough to cause substantial damage were ever experienced in that part of the world. Soon after, a heavy windstorm caused a resounding loss to the overseas subsidiary. The loss would have been collectible under a U.S. extended coverage insurance contract.

Another story, probably apocryphal, involves a U.S. risk manager who reported to his overseas insurer the installation of sprinklers in the company's overseas plant. He expected to receive a reduction in the fire insurance rate, but instead received an invoice for additional premium to cover the increased hazard of sprinkler leakage!

Individual and Syndication Bases

Beginning in the mid-1950s, some property insurers, generally of U.S., British, or Italian origin, took steps to help overcome these problems. Two approaches were used—individual and syndication. In the individual method, a large insurer would obtain authority to operate in several countries other than its country of origin, thus permitting it to serve its corporate insureds on a multinational basis.

In syndication, insurers from different countries of origin joined together to provide insurance protection to the corporate insured. Coverage was as identical as possible to that enjoyed by the U.S. corporate insured in the U.S., to the extent permitted by the laws or regulations of the countries involved. Whether an individual or a syndicated basis was used, it was necessary to use the forms of coverage prescribed by the countries in which the property was located. Invariably, a "difference in conditions" policy would then be written specifying that, if any of the coverages provided in the insurance policies issued to the overseas subsidiaries did not equal the coverage of a U.S. property insurance contract, then the difference in conditions contract would respond.

In addition to standardizing coverage, this blanketing arrangement often resulted in premium savings because the insurer or syndicate could treat all of the properties involved as one risk, to the extent permitted by the laws and regulations of the countries in which the properties were located.

Most corporate risk managers regard formation of an offshore captive insurer a refinement of this blanketing arrangement offered by individual multinationally admitted insurers or syndicates of insurers.

The Do-It-Yourself Approach

The captive approach permits the corporate parent to accomplish a greater degree of do-it-yourself risk bearing than most any other form of insurance mechanism. In those countries where the local laws permit it, and there are many, the risk can be insured directly with the captive insurer. The premium flowing from an overseas operating subsidiary to the captive insurer is an expense on the books of the operating subsidiary in calculating the tax it owes to its country of origin.

In those countries where local law or custom makes this direct approach difficult or impossible, then a locally admitted insurer is asked to insure the corporate parent's property within that country. This locally admitted insurer can then reinsure a portion of the risk with the corporate parent's offshore captive insurer. This reinsurance treaty would have to provide enough remuneration to the locally admitted insurer to reimburse it for any local services, claims handling, and other expenses, plus a reasonable profit.

There are countries, notably in South and Central America, that limit the amount of reinsurance which can be exported from the country, or prohibit it entirely. In these instances, the above described arrangement is more difficult.

In the case of Ford Motor Company, the IRS sought to deny a tax deduction for property insurance coverage that an overseas subsidiary paid to Ford's offshore captive insurer. The case was settled (without an opinion being issued) with enough satisfaction to the taxpayer to conclude that favorable tax treatment still exists, at least until the ramifications of the Service's "economic family" theory becomes more evident, a subject we shall address later.

The overseas casualty risks of U.S. corporations can be insured in the offshore captive insurance company, the same as property risks. However, this use of the captive has not been pursued as vigorously. One reason may be that, in the U.S., the high dollar volume of casualty coverage is workers' compensation, while overseas this coverage is generally provided by the government and not through insurance. The remaining overseas casualty coverages, at least until recently, were relatively so low in cost that the existing arrangement was not disturbed.

This situation may be changing due to the burgeoning product liability risks arising in some countries. Recently the risk manager of a large U.S. based multinational was wrestling with the problem of responsibility for potential liability on a product manufactured in France, under specifications of the U.S. company, and marketed in Spain by the company's Spanish subsidiary. This type of situation cries out for one insurance policy completely under the company's control, with in-house determination of culpability, rather than through the efforts of three insurers.

Tax Free if Not Repatriated

An attractive feature of the captive insurer arrangement as to overseas, i.e., non U.S. risks, is that federal income, both underwriting and investment, is free of U.S. federal income tax as long as it is not repatriated to the U.S. parent. If and when these earnings are repatriated to the U.S. parent, then the corporation's regular tax rate applies. This is not a tax exemption but a tax deferral. I emphasize this because the more ardent proponents of the offshore captive insurer concept have a tendency to describe this as a tax-free arrangement, which it is not.

One such advocate, after reluctantly conceding that this was actually a tax deferral, contended that the typical U.S. corporate parent would never have to repatriate its captive insurer's earnings, and thus, in effect, this arrangement would be tax-free. I observed that never is a very long time.

It should be noted that, if a corporation places insurance in its overseas subsidiary, the federal government collects a four percent sales tax for the privilege of exporting the premium. If an insurer does the exporting, a one percent excise tax applies.

Capacity Crunch Injects New Life

The first U.S. captives were probably the mutual insurance companies developed by groups of manufacturers and other business persons in the late nineteenth and early twentieth centuries to take care of particular, specialized risks to which these developers were subject. The names of these mutuals describe their origin and their purpose—manufacturers, lumbermens, hardware, and threshermens. Most of these are either gone or have entered the conventional insurance market.

The insurance capacity crunch of 1973 to 1975 brought new life into the captive insurer concept. One coverage particularly affected by the shortage of insurance capacity was medical and hospital malpractice, which gave a powerful impetus to the formation of insurers sponsored by groups of hospitals and doctors. Some of these insurers were formed offshore; others were formed domestically. This phenomenon is similar to the formation of the mutuals in earlier years. Both are products of persons determined to solve a problem on a do-it-yourself basis. Domestically, these insurers must adhere to the same federal tax code that all other insurers adhere to.

Colorado and Tennessee enacted legislation designed to facilitate the establishment of captive insurers. Their requirements are favorable compared with requirements to form a normal insurer in other states. Relatively few insurers have been formed under the Colorado and Tennessee enactments and opinions differ as to how favorable these requirements are when compared to the requirements of Bermuda or the Grand Cayman Islands. However, in mid-1981, the State of Vermont enacted the Special Insurers Act enabling captive company formation. In terms of a domestic situs, it offers the most favorable climate for U.S. corporations with primarily U.S. based exposures.

A Surge in Offshore Captives

Many insurance coverages other than medical and hospital malpractice were in extremely short supply during the mid-1970s. Product liability coverage, particularly for hard goods manufacturers such as machinery and machine tools became extremely difficult to obtain. This situation gave rise to the formation of hundreds of offshore insurers by U.S. corporations and trade associations. This surge still continues. Corporations and others who had formed or sponsored captive insurers primarily to insure property risks began using these insurers to secure casualty coverages.

Property insurance coverage is relatively easy to export to an offshore insurance facility, as far as state or other regulatory authority is concerned. Liability insurance tends to be difficult and workers' compensation is impossible to accomplish. However, the ultimate objective was accomplished by insuring the risk with a U.S. insurer licensed to write the risk, with a provision that a substantial part of the risk be reinsured in the captive insurer owned or controlled by the party susceptible to the risk.

IRS Ruling 77–316

The IRS, through its Revenue Ruling 77–316, has announced that it will challenge the tax deductibility of premiums which have not left the "economic family" of the taxpayer, no matter whether the premium went directly into the captive or via the reinsurance route through a licensed U.S. insurer. It should be noted that, while Ruling 77–316 dealt with situations involving offshore captives, it later indicated its position was the same for domestic captives.

This economic family theory is based on an obscure court case. It involves an aged woman, whose attempt to insure herself with a whole life insurance policy and simultaneously with an annuity contract, was held not to have transferred the risk to the insurer. I believe this theory has been applied by the IRS only to this type of situation. No such language exists in the tax statutes, which contain fairly straightforward language such as "reasonable and necessary expense."

The attempt by the IRS to introduce this economic family restriction into the tax law will not go unchallenged. The Carnation Company case, which was recently won by the Service, in tax court and upon appeal, denied tax deductibility on the facts determined by the court and not on the economic family theory. It is true that the appeals court mentioned the economic family theory but only by way of dicta, that is, by a sort of offhand observation by the court, not used to actually determine the outcome of the case.

Multi-Owner Captives

Whether or not the IRS position on the economic family theory will prevail is not now known. What it has done, however, is increase the interest in multi-owner captives by members of associations and other groups. By merging one's risks with those of others, the economic family no longer exists.

In addition, if properly structured, the multi-owned captive could become a noncontrolled foreign company even though completely owned by U.S. interests. This is often achieved by providing that no shareholder has more than 10 percent of the ownership, since this is the percentage used in attributing ownership for tax purposes in a controlled foreign corporation. A noncontrolled foreign corporation pays no federal income tax. This could be especially advantageous where so-called long tail coverages such as product liability, professional liability, even workers' compensation, are concerned.

No matter how inviting or attractive the tax advantage seems to be, experience would indicate that, somewhere along the line, the IRS stands waiting to extract the appropriate tax.

Can a corporate parent place any of its U.S. risks in its offshore captive insurer without the insurer incurring a federal tax liability; and, if so, to what extent? The answer to the first part of this question is yes. To describe the extent, we must pick our way carefully through the appropriate sections of the tax code together with the regulations amplifying these sections of the code.

Under a rule of law called "de minimis" applied to Section 953 (a) of the Internal Revenue Code, as much as five percent of the captive insurer's total premiums may be derived from its parent's risks located within or from operations arising wholly within the United States, and still not affect the captive insurer's favorable tax treatment. If more than five percent of premium is derived from U.S. risks, the income derived from this amount in excess of five percent is said to be tainted, and U.S. federal income tax is levied on this excess amount. Investment earnings from reserves arising from these U.S. risks (in excess of five percent) are likewise tainted and are subject to U.S. federal taxation as such.

Raising 5% to 75%

By surrendering 100 percent ownership in the offshore insurer, the U.S. corporate parent may increase this five percent limitation. If the U.S. corporate parent owns (directly or indirectly—under rules of attribution or constructive ownership) no more than 25 percent of the offshore captive's stock, then this five percent limitation is raised to 75 percent. This is explicitly permitted in Section 957 (a) and (b) of the tax code governing a "controlled foreign corporation," the provisions of which come into play once the five percent de minimis limitation has been breached.

The 25 percent to 75 percent ratio is the threshold where the tax code (Section 957 (b)) exempts the U.S. corporate parent repatriating its share of the foreign insurer's income. All experts seem to agree, however, that the remaining 75 percent of the insurer's ownership (or at least 50 percent) has to be of a non-U.S. character to escape the provisions of subpart F of these tax provisions.

Let us assume that a U.S. corporation placed some of its U.S. risks with a foreign insurer in which the corporation had 26 percent or more ownership interest or control. Would this mean that the U.S. corporation would have to pay U.S. income tax on all earnings it derived from the foreign insurer? The answer to this is no. Only those earnings are taxable which cannot be eliminated by one or more of the tax provisions permitting this tax deferral.

It should be further understood that there may well be certain insurance risks of the U.S. corporate parent which may logically be construed to be only partly applicable to activities within the United States, such as marine insurance on company-owned ships which travel to many ports of the world, including U.S. ports. For these and similar instances, certain criteria (length of time in the U.S., etc.) have been developed over the years which define what are U.S. transactions and what are not. In addition, the tax code has other provisions which come into play to reduce the tainted income and to minimize the tax. There is, for instance, a provision that shields from U.S. tax any unrelated investment income of the insurer if it amounts to less than 30 percent of the gross underwriting and investment results.

Possible Tax Deferral

All of the benefits of forming a captive insurer can be and often are available in the formation of a domestic captive insurer. These benefits are economy of serving the risks, the ability to tailor the coverages to the needs of the corporate parent, and achieving volume discounts on the risks ultimately placed with the conventional insurance market. In the case of the offshore captive insurer, one must add to the benefit the possible deferral of U.S. federal tax liability, if the captive insurer is organized in one of the tax haven countries, such as Bermuda, which assesses a nominal tax at most on the insurer's operations. Another possible advantage of incorporating in a country such as Bermuda is that a minimal amount of supervision over these insurers is required. This absence of supervision provides great flexibility to the insurer in its writing and its operations. It offers the opportunity to write coverages which are difficult or impossible to obtain from the conventional insurance market.

17

Employee Benefits and the Corporate Risk Manager

The risk manager's responsibility for the corporate employee benefits program varies from company to company. Generally speaking, the larger the corporation, the less responsibility the risk manager has for determining the benefits that will be offered and administering the benefits adopted. Typically, the risk manager is responsible for purchasing the insurance involved, while the personnel or industrial relations department determines what the employee benefits of the company shall be, and administers the day-to-day program.

Benefits as Compensation

Under the Wagner Act, most employee benefits are considered items of compensation subject to negotiation between the company and its unions; thus the logic of involving personnel or industrial relations. Also, employees and company alike regard the company's contribution to employee benefits as closely related to wages and salaries.

By having the risk manager assume responsibility for purchasing insurance, the corporation is likely to benefit from volume purchase. And it centers in one department the coordination with and evaluation of the insurance industry on behalf of the corporation. Obviously, the risk manager who can competently negotiate and purchase the corporate property and casualty insurance coverages, can do likewise for the employee benefits program.

Accounting for Employee Benefits

In many corporations the risk management department handles the accounting for employee benefits. This is logical because, in most cases, the risk management function is a part of the finance department. Preparation of accounting entries requires intimate knowledge of the elements underlying insurance company charges for services performed.

In small companies, particularly those whose production employees are not unionized, the risk manager is often responsible for administering the employee benefits program.

Whether or not assigned responsibility, risk managers ought to familiarize themselves with employee benefits programs because they involve uncertainty and risk to the company.

Little Shifting of Risk

Even though nearly all employee benefits programs have underlying insurance contracts, there is surprisingly little shifting of risk to insurers. Rather, the trend is toward retrospectively rated insurance contracts which provide that, after payment of benefits to an employee and a charge for the insurer's services, called the insurer's retention, any money left over from the premium is returned in the form of a retrospective credit, called a *retro credit.* If the losses paid or incurred are greater than expected, resulting in a retrospective debit, the employer is expected to reimburse the insurer for this deficiency. In other words, these contracts are really cost-plus in nature, with the actual risk of loss borne by the employer.

The typical insurance program is written with one insurer on a blanket retrospective basis, which means that if one line of insurance, say life, goes into deficit, the redundancy in any other line will be used by the insurer to eliminate the deficiency.

Small Firms Prefer Fixed Cost

Not all employee benefit contracts between corporations and insurers are written on a cost plus basis. Small companies with relatively few employees prefer a fixed cost type of contract, in which the insurer will charge a certain amount per employee or per family for each month of protection. Thus, the insurer bears the risk of excessive losses. The insurer generally guarantees that these rates will not change during the policy term, which can be for three years but more often is for one year.

Even the largest of corporations may have a fixed cost type contract for such benefits as accidental death and dismemberment coverage, where the benefits paid are extremely high in relation to the premiums paid. Also some medical reimbursement plans, notably those provided by Blue Cross and Blue Shield, provide benefits by and large on a fixed cost basis. In so doing, these organizations spread the risk of hospital, surgical and other medical costs throughout the entire community.

The View of the "Blues"

The "blues," as they are known by the health insurance world, believe this arrangement is more desirable from a social point of view than a retrospectively rated arrangement under which the employees of each corporation, rather than the community, take care of their own medical expenses.

The conventional insurers believe experience-rated medical reimbursement plans represent sound underwriting judgment. It is rare that a corporation does not consider its employees and their families a better risk than the general population.

Whether the "blues" or the conventional insurers are justified in their attitudes depends on whether their actions are regarded as sound underwriting or as cream skimming. This distinction is important in virtually every line of insurance offered by the industry. For instance, is it sound underwriting or cream skimming to offer an experience rated plan, excluding people 65 and over, in which the participants collectively pay the medical expenses of those who become ill? People 65 and over have twice as many illnesses, three times as severe, as people under 65. Is it proper to give the group under 65 the benefit of their better experience? Or does such a device discriminate against those over 65?

Fundamental Fair Play

Obviously any such grouping must be legal and must not violate what the public regards as fundamental fair play. Beyond that it becomes a matter of judgment and enlightened self interest. Further, if high social purpose is served by prohibiting such groupings for loss-sharing purposes, then such prohibition should be legislated. It should be recognized that if the legislative process provides for a broadly based risk sharing device, such as a universal health plan covering the entire populace, the legislators are, in fact, stipulating that the total costs involved are best borne by broader groups. This is the legislators' right to do, subject always to the constitutional guarantees to the individuals involved.

It should also be understood that if a segment within the group pays more than it would through the conventional insurance market, because its losses are lower, the additional payment is, in effect, a tax, rather than an insurance premium.

I look with disfavor at any taxing scheme dressed up as an insurance plan. The insuring mechanism has enough weaknesses of its own to answer for without taking on the ill favor associated with a tax collecting device. As Edmund Burke said, "To tax and to please, no more than to love and to be wise, is not given to men."

The Makeup of Typical Benefit Plans

What does the typical corporate employee benefits program look like? There is a lock-step uniformity among corporations, for several reasons. What is customary has great weight among people who develop employee benefits. There are tax considerations both for the corporation and for the individual employee. The product line of insurers marketing employee benefits also has an influence. Differences are in detail and not in substance.

This uniformity is understandable. No corporate management wants to lag behind other corporations with whom it competes for personnel. Also top managements of corporations are prudent, conservative individuals, who are persuaded in large degree by what competitors, or their industry as a whole, are offering.

It is the rare corporation today that does not have some form of group life insurance for its employees, with the benefit varying in relation to the employees' annual salary levels. It may range from one times annual salary to three times annual salary, and more. Two times is probably the most common. The amount of this benefit, unfortunately, is not determined according to need, but rather according to how much the employees are able or willing to pay and how much the company can afford.

Until the mid-1950s, virtually all group life insurance programs terminated coverage upon the employee's retirement. The logic behind this approach is that the principal reason for life insurance is to provide for the exigencies arising from *premature* death. It could be argued that an employee, having attained retirement status, could not suffer premature death.

Despite this logic, it's become customary for corporations to provide post retirement group life insurance. It was invariably computed as a percentage (ranging from 100 percent to 10 percent) of the benefit enjoyed by the employee while active. The amount was usually modified by the employee's seniority with the company.

If group life insurance is the keystone in the typical corporation's employee benefits program, an accident and sickness indemnity insurance plan is not far behind. Several states require that employers provide some form of this benefit to their employees within the state. These plans pay a weekly benefit to disabled employees, calculated as a percent of their salary. The term of this benefit is generally 26 weeks, with some form of waiting period, ranging from three days to seven days, before the benefit becomes applicable.

As popular as life and accident and sickness, is insurance for medical expenses of employees and their families. The kind and extent of expense eligible for reimbursement are diverse and follow no logical or consistent pattern.

Retirement Benefits

The fourth major benefit necessary to meet the minimum needs of employees is a retirement benefit. This benefit is generally calculated by one of two methods or by a combination of the two. The first is sometimes called the steel formula, because it originated in a union contract negotiated in that industry.

This benefit provides that the retiree receive a set sum of dollars of retirement income per month for each year of service. Since the typical employee's career is about 25 years, such plans provide a monthly retirement benefit of 25 times this set sum.

Another formula often used is in the form of an annuity, the cost of which was accumulated during the employee's career with the company. For example, if a corporation's plan provides a two percent benefit on career average earnings, the employee with 25 years of service and average earnings of $10,000 a year, would receive a benefit at retirement of $5,000 a year. Due to inflationary pressures, in recent years many plans have incorporated a "final earnings" feature which is used in determining monthly retirement benefits.

In addition to these four employee benefits coverages, some corporations offer some form of additional death and dismemberment insurance. An increasingly popular benefit is group long term disability insurance. It provides a payment, generally computed as a percent of the employee's salary, ranging from 40 to 65 percent, if the employee should suffer serious sickness or accident. Payment is continued as long as the employee is unable to work.

Who Pays How Much?

An important consideration in all of these employee benefits is how much the corporation will pay, and how much the employee will pay. There is no uniformity. Many corporations pay virtually the entire bill, while others pay none.

The trend, if any, is toward the employer paying more and more.

A reason often cited for this involves the federal tax code. The employer who pays for these coverages may deduct the cost as a business expense on the corporate tax return. So, if the employer is operating at a profit, the federal government, in effect, absorbs about half the cost. If the employer were to pay the identical sum to the employee in the form of salary, and the employee then proceeded to pay for the employee benefits, the employer would still receive the same federal tax deduction. But the employee would have to pay income tax on the added salary. This is a powerful stimulus for employee benefits to be paid, not by employees, but by employers.

Theoretically, if an employee were paying for a benefit costing $10 per month, the employer could agree to pay the employee $12 a month less (assuming the employee is in a 20 percent tax bracket). The end result would be that the employee would receive the same net income, while the employer's after-tax cost was reduced by the 20 percent.

We may wonder why employers don't pay virtually all employee benefits. One powerful deterrent is that payment of an employee benefit is a long term commitment. Once an employer agrees to pay for it, it is extremely difficult, if not impossible, to withdraw it. If profits should disappear, the employer would still be expected to pay for the benefits, even though there were no profits against which the costs of the employee benefit could be applied.

Uniformity Required

Another deterrent to the employer paying all is that an employee benefit must be extended to all employees on a uniform basis. This uniformity of benefits to eligible employees is the very essence of the group benefits concept. But it does introduce a complication often solved by leaving the employee benefits on an employee-pay basis.

To illustrate, let's take group life insurance. An employee who is the parent of a number of dependent children would undoubtedly welcome a group life insurance benefit of five times annual salary, especially if the employer pays all. But what about employees who have no dependents? These employees will probably not be so enthusiastic about the huge group life insurance benefit. They would probably be considerably less than enthusiastic if they realized they were receiving less in their paychecks to help pay the cost of the benefit for others.

Thus, by putting the employee benefit on an employee-pay basis, the employer has greater flexibility. The single employee with no after-death liabilities, and the employee with grown children may elect not to participate in the program and, instead, use the money saved to provide something more in keeping with their personal needs. This flexibility would be impossible if the employer had decided to pay employees through the employee benefit route rather than through the paycheck.

Where Your Money Goes

Imagine yourself an employee of a corporation with a typical employee benefits program. Envision what you do with the money you receive in your paycheck. You pay for food, shelter, recreation for yourself and your family. You pay for the care and education of your children. Your automobile and house are ultimately paid, for the most part, out of your paycheck.

In this exercise we should not ignore those items which we never get our hands on because they represent salary withheld. Probably the largest item of withholding is for federal and state taxes. Then there are social security payments, and contributions to various employee benefits programs and the like. This exercise should dramatize how all pervasive is the force of the money paid to us for our services.

For every dollar we receive in our paychecks, another quarter to a third of a dollar is paid out by our employers for so-called fringe benefits. First comes the employer's contribution to the federal Social Security fund. By this we are assured of a pension and payment for medical attention under Medicare when we reach retirement age, a payment to our spouse or under-age children if we should die prematurely, and monthly payments to ourselves if we should become disabled before reaching retirement age. Our employer's contribution is equal to our own contribution.

If we become unemployed we can receive unemployment compensation for as long as 26 weeks, supplemented in times of recession by government grants for longer periods. Depending on the state, the cost can be as low as $50.00 but can go up to much higher amounts.

Virtually all of us are protected by workers' compensation in our state. If we should suffer injury or death in a work-connected injury, we or our spouse and under-age children will receive indemnity for the medical expenses incurred, plus a payment in lieu of the salary lost due to the accidental injury.

All of these benefit programs are mandatory. We and our employer are required by law to belong and contribute. The remainder of this associated payroll expense is made up of the employer's voluntary payments for group life insurance, group hospital, surgical and other medical insurance, and retirement benefits.

By comparing your paycheck with these associated payroll expenses, you would learn that these expenses often total as much as one-third of your paycheck. Few people would perceive the value received through these expenses to be in line with what they cost.

Stupendous Waste

The conclusion seems inescapable that there is stupendous waste in this whole area of providing employee benefits. I do not mean that those who are responsible for developing and administering the benefit plans are wasteful or extravagant in their work. Whether they be in government agencies or in private corporations, most of those I have met are conscientious, intelligent and industrious and have a keen dedication to their work. Perhaps it is this dedication which makes it difficult for these people to have an overview of the entire employee benefits picture.

I think it is time to come down to earth and seek more concrete data. What follows, while not necessarily proving my contention, may serve at least as an outline for further study of this extremely important question, namely the amount of financial resources, whether in government or private programs, that should be allocated to employee benefits, how these resources should be spent, and who should do the administering.

Coordination of Benefits

A risk manager friend of mine presents this exercise:

Assume that a middle-aged male employee dies. Under the company group life insurance plan, his widow is entitled to a benefit of $50,000, equal to twice the employee's annual salary. She and her under-age children are entitled to survivor's benefits under the Social Security program. The benefit can vary greatly in amount, but let us assume its present value is equal to the group insurance benefit.

Let us further assume that workers' compensation benefits were also collectible, due to the nature of the employee's death. In many states the present value of this benefit can equal $100,000, thus doubling the amount to which the widow and children are entitled.

Suppose further, that the employee died while on a business trip and the company has a travel accident insurance policy providing a benefit equal to two years pay. Other employee benefits could also become payable here, such as an accidental death and dismemberment benefit, a surviving spouse's benefit paid in conjunction with the company pension plan, a special insurance payment if the company plane is involved.

No one begrudges this widow the benefits she will receive which would, in our hypothetical case, equal to eight to ten times her late husband's annual salary. She has suffered a great loss and now has the heavy responsibility of raising her family without her husband's income and other help.

But we must strive for the necessary detachment to ask what about the wives and surviving children of those employees who die prematurely of natural causes? These families may have to get along with the group life and Social Security benefits only. These would be considerably less than what the first family will receive. Why should the circumstances of how a person dies determine the amount of benefits to be received by dependents?

Every person engaged in employee benefits planning, estate planning and the like, agrees that benefits payable upon a person's death should best be measured by the amount of financial responsibility left by the deceased.

A detached review would suggest, I think, that perhaps greater equity would be served if benefits were designed to be paid more on the basis of need and less on happenstance. It is impossible to estimate and difficult to guess how much this duplication of benefits adds to the total employee benefits bill of the nation. It is obvious, however, that a logical system of benefit payments would result in more responsive benefits or that such benefits would take less of the employee benefits dollar, or both. Certainly these are desirable goals.

Jurisdictional Conflicts

Every corporate risk manager has probably had to work out the details of a jurisdictional conflict involving whether a disabled employee is entitled to collect under the state sponsored workers' compensation program or under the non work connected disability benefits insurance programs.

Normally, the details of a specific jurisdictional problem are simple enough to resolve. An employee claims for indemnity payments under one of these programs, either for lost earnings while disabled or for medical expenses. Usually this is done under the non work-connected disability benefits insurance program. At some time during the insurer's investigation to determine if the employee is eligible for benefits, evidence is discovered that the employee's disability is work connected.

The disability insurance excludes payment under such circumstances. The insurer suspends payments and the employee must now proceed to establish a claim under the state sponsored workers' compensation program. The ultimate decision of whether workers' compensation coverage is applicable is made by the state's compensation commission which has administrative and quasijudicial powers to make such a determination.

Spending $5,000 to "Save" $100

In most cases, the difference in benefits paid under either insurance plan is not substantial, since the majority of cases involves a temporary disability. After one such case in which two hearings were held before a compensation commission hearing officer (which must have cost the insurer and insured a minimum of $5,000, since four employees, including an attorney, had to spend several days attending it), it developed that less than $100 more would have been paid to the employee under workers' compensation than under the insured's (non work connected) accident and sickness and medical reimbursement insurance programs.

We wonder who exactly is being served by this lack of coordination, with the expense of administering two investigations, two insurers each maintaining records, etc. Why should an employee be paid differently for lost income or medical expense reimbursement by virtue of some detail, often obscure, as to the cause?

Note that in the examples cited above there is no duplication of benefits paid to the disabled employee from these two programs of reimbursement for lost income. The duplication lies in the administration of two separate plans and the duplication of overhead expense.

Those defenders of the present workers' compensation system who argue that this system charges back to the hazardous industry the losses found only in that industry, should look more closely at workers' compensation losses being paid under that program. I think they will find that, in most instances, the losses so paid resemble those for injuries and other disabilities found among the population generally, rather than those applicable to the industry in which the employer is engaged.

Most Fatal Accidents are Off-the-Job

Of the 16,000-plus deaths annually from industrial accidents, less than 2,000 are actually attributable to the plant or factory environment. The remaining 14,000 are caused by auto accidents and similar off-the-job causes.

The cost of those accidents applicable to the activities of a specific industry could still be allocated specifically to that industry on a system of indemnification which combined both industrial and non-industrial disabilities. This would leave the other incidences of disability more attributable to the population generally. On-the-job heart attacks, automobile accidents while on company business, or other accidents, the cause of which cannot really be attributed to the particular work environment of the employee, could then be handled consistently and less expensively in one plan which would not spend dollars unnecessarily determining whether or not the disabilities were work-connected.

The duplication, the triplication and worse, is found everywhere in this area of income replacement or medical expense indemnification, but particularly in income replacement. There is, of course, the state workers' compensation systems and the federal Social Security system. Many companies, either voluntarily or by agreement with their employees' unions, have plans supplementing the payments from these governmental entities in addition to such payments.

The Waste of Multiplicity

The waste—there is no other word for it—caused by this duplication of administrative machinery, plus the nonstandardization of procedures and data required of these multiplicity of plans, would astound us all if it could be accurately calculated. The lack of standardization of benefits, procedures and other administrative detail among the 50 states and the District of Columbia is notorious. To multistate employers and the insurers servicing them, it is an expensive burden.

At least five states have compulsory non-work connected disability benefits insurance,l with niggling differences in benefits and administrative apparatus. The corporate employer with widespread multistate operations typically has not five such plans but six—five mandatory and one of its own (or its insurer's) creation for the remaining states in which it operates.

Is there any useful justification for the different states to require different rates and different procedures in their programs? The federal Social Security program is still different, while the five states with the compulsory non-work connected disability coverage have still different reporting criteria.

The typical employee, when caught in the middle of these inconsistencies, has very little sympathy for or understanding of the situation. This duplication and nonstandardization might be endured if the overall result was a consistently good job for the people these plans are designed to benefit.

Is a National Health Insurance Plan the Answer?

Powerful voices are claiming that this is not being done. These voices are centered in Washington, D.C., and they purport to have the answer—a national health plan for the entire population, providing indemnity for hospital, surgical, and other medical expenses through the federal Social Security program, together with continued amplification of the indemnification of lost income through that Social Security program, all to be administered by the federal government.

Such a monolithic program would be bad for the intended beneficiaries, their employers and, yes, for the federal government. It would be a disaster for the insurance industry. Does it not make sense for all who have a responsibility in this area, whether insurer, risk manager, employee benefits manager, and state insurance supervisory staff to work, to make sense out of this jerrybuilt area of corporate activity?

Government or Private Control?

In reviewing the overall employee benefits picture in this country today, we find a problem difficult to solve. Should the various aspects of benefits be under the control of government, with government not only supervising the activity, but assessing the population generally or the specific class of people benefiting, for the cost of maintaining the activity?

Or should benefits continue to be maintained more or less on a voluntary basis, with the participants voluntarily assessing themselves?

There are many areas of human activity which, practically speaking, can only be maintained by government. If the government had to sell these activities, in a manner similar to private industry selling its products or service, sales costs would probably far exceed the income the government would receive from the relatively few who would voluntarily pay their share.

As an example, take the Democratic Party. After losing a recent Presidential election, it attempted to reduce its campaign deficit through a series of television appeals. The result was a fiasco. The party didn't receive enough response to pay for the television broadcasts. I would guess that the federal government would have the same problem if it attempted to sell many of its programs.

Medicare Prime Example

Some thoughtful students on the subject believe the government's Medicare program to be in this category. They believe that people over 65 will not or cannot pay enough to meet the cost of the medical bills, etc., of the group. It is necessary, therefore, that the whole group be enrolled and the whole group assessed, thus eliminating the sales cost.

Peter Drucker made a good point when he said that the most precious thing about private enterprise is the fact that it will fail if it has ceased to meet the objective for which it was formed, while government programs are almost impossible to destruct. As soon as these government programs are brought into being, they immediately create special groups and special interests who work hard to keep these programs going long after they have outlived their usefulness.

The correct mix of government sponsored, tax supported programs on the one hand, and a program involving voluntary participation and voluntary payment on the other hand, is most important. Attaining this mix in the employee benefits field is indeed well worth continued and intensive study.

Self Insured or Captive?

Quite often the question arises whether or not employee benefits can be self insured. The answer is yes, but there are special problems involved in such handling of employee benefits. While it is open to debate, at least one attorney whose judgment I trust implicitly has expressed the opinion that no plan in which employee benefits are involved should be self insured unless there is some specific statutory authority that permits it, such as the California Disability Benefits Law.

On the other hand, I've heard other erudite persons express the opinion that the acceptance of employee contributions on the books of the corporation represents no particular problem, as long as adequate records are maintained.

What Is a "Plan"?

There have been enough government administrative decisions, primarily by the U.S. Treasury Department, to assure us that, if the self insured arrangement of the employer is in fact a plan, then the payments made to that plan are deductible for tax purposes, and will not be construed as additional income to the employees. To effect such an arrangement, a "plan" must be published generally among the participants, it must not discriminate and it must be administered fairly and consistently.

One particular aspect of the Internal Revenue Code permits a payment up to $5,000 to the family of a deceased employee without it being assumed that the payment is compensation. This could suggest that any self insured plan providing a death benefit in excess of $5,000 could result in such excess being construed as taxable income paid by the employer and, as such, subject to income tax payable by the estate of the deceased employee.

I find no evidence that there has been any appreciable ground swell toward establishing captive insurance companies to provide benefits to employees of large corporations. The concept has been discussed. And a smattering of corporations have acquired life insurance companies. Invariably these corporations have indicated that the life insurer they acquired was in fact seen as a profit center. As such it would appear that it could not be defined as a captive insurance company.

It's my understanding that some captives have accepted reinsurance from a domestic insurer who insures the captive owner's domestic risks. The IRS has challenged the tax deductibility of this on the same "economic family" theory that we described in the discussion of captive insurers. This novel theory propounded by IRS cannot, at this time, be the subject of intelligent discussion.

Protecting Key Personnel

Closely allied to employee benefits is a type of insurance that covers the loss of management people on whom the success of the corporation heavily rests. It is usually called key-man insurance.

Sometimes the corporation opts to obtain coverage for key executives. But more often it is required by a bank or other lending institution which has made loans to the corporation. If the key person should die prematurely, the proceeds of the insurance are used to tide the corporation over the difficult period until the key manager's position is suitably filled.

Since the corporation is the beneficiary, the premiums paid for this insurance are a deductible expense on the corporate tax return. However, if the life insurance contract is of the cash value type with a cash surrender value built up over the years, the tax authorities, as well as the rules of good accounting practice, require that the cash surrender portion of the premium be treated as an asset which is recoverable from the insurance company.

18

The Business/Academic Community Interface

As we have seen, risk management evolved from corporate insurance management and the proper make-up and administration of a corporate insurance portfolio still constitutes a substantial part of the risk manager's responsibility.

Yet within the academic world there is an overwhelming emphasis on *insurance* and consequently a minimal emphasis on *risk.* The courses taught, the reading material assigned, and thus the student theses are primarily devoted to the actions and interactions between and among insurers, insureds and insurance intermediaries. Study is devoted to what to do with the risk—how much to charge for transferring the risk, how insurers are regulated by state authority, and similar insurance-oriented activities. About 99 percent of the time, after the risk is identified, academicians assume that it will be passed on to an insurance company. Time is spent teaching where the insurance broker, or agent fits into this process, but here, too, the emphasis is on the insuring aspect and not the risk per se.

Academia Advanced Risk Concept

Curiously enough, it was the academic world that insisted that the business world must broaden its horizons and think of risk—how to measure it, how to eliminate it, or how to effectively neutralize it by other means—only one of these means being to transfer the risk to an insurer. I think it is no exaggeration to say that the academicians dragged the insurance industry kicking and screaming to this broader concept. Having done this, they promptly left us, unclothed and shivering, in this advanced posture as the corporate risk experts.

They continue to send to us graduates who are insurance-transferring technicians rather than risk analysis specialists. Consider how few insurance graduates have really been exposed to industrial safety or loss prevention. Few of them can explain what the Z16A index is, or identify it as a major index used to determine industrial accident frequency and severity. Few of these graduates could tell what an explosion proof roof is, even if one fell on them. Few could be sure whether the Walsh-Healey Act is a new television comedy team or the sponsors of the first effective federal law outlining standards of industrial plant safety conditions.

Most Graduates Become Brokers

There are good reasons for this situation. I was told by the department head of an eastern seaboard university that 80 percent of his graduates who major in insurance go into insurance agency/ brokerage work, 17 to 18 percent take jobs in insurance companies and a stray two or three percent take jobs in corporate insurance or risk management departments. So it isn't difficult to understand the emphasis in the university curriculum on insurance marketing action and interaction, with consequent deemphasis of risk in its pure aspects.

I do not condemn this emphasis, but I would ask the universities to consider recent trends in the insurance industry and in the business world.

Surely but fitfully, and sometimes painfully, the present conventional insurance industry is broadening itself into what eventually must be the financial services business. This is a fascinating evolution, involving the insurance industry maneuvering to enter the securities business, mutual funds, and who knows—perhaps credit cards, banking and what have you. The academic world must respond to this evolutionary process. Whether it will do so in a constructive way is still open to question.

Corporate Risks Increase

The evolutionary process in the business world is more complicated. With increases of population, developing technology, increase in governmental activity, rising expectations and similar forces, the corporate world faces a dramatic increase in pure, nonspeculative risks. These risks are fortuitous in nature, not controllable by person or corporation. Yet they are not insurable, primarily because there is no one around to insure them. Let's take a couple of examples:

Case Number 1

In companies selling or trading securities, an increase in surveillance by the Securities and Exchange Commission of the employees actually doing the trading or selling has caused many of these firms to establish the position of *compliance officer.* The job is to see that all appropriate employees have been informed of the rules under which they are to operate and, equally important, to make sure that corporate records show that the employees have acknowledged being advised of such rules. The compliance officer also assures that such rules are being observed in the operation of the firm. This activity, in essence, is the ascertainment and disposition of a fortuitous, nonspeculative, nonbusiness risk, as much as any such risk included in a corporate insurance program.

Case Number 2

Within the last ten years many airlines, beset by organized thievery of cargo and baggage, and many large department store chains with substantial instantly usable inventories on hand, have placed a vice president of security on the payroll. What is the difference, as far as risk ascertainment and risk disposition is concerned, between loss of material by theft and loss of material by fire?

Under the definitions which the academicians have supplied, both of the above should fall within the scope of the risk manager's job.

Conflicting Trends Within the Academic Community

There appears to be two distinct trends emerging in the academic community. One that is positive in nature is the growing emphasis on the risk aspect of our business. At least one major university, located in the southeast, now has a risk management department, headed by a full professor. The increase in fortuitous risks these days should serve to emphasize the need for more research on pure risk. This emphasis on risk expresses itself in another way. Risk management is now appearing as a subject for study and discussion in courses of a general nature such as accounting, finance and similar courses. This is a positive development.

Yet in more and more colleges and universities, the officials who develop curricula have challenged the concept that insurance should be retained as a major course of study, citing their belief that it is in fact a technical area somewhat akin to preparation for a real estate license examination and should be offered as such. The diminution of this study cannot be helpful to the continued advance of our specialty.

It is ironic that the premier sciences of our specialty, risk assessment and probability, are taught under the tutelage of the mathematics department.

One such department of a prestigious eastern university now offers a seminar in risk assessment and probability to business people. Well over 90 percent of attendees supporting this program are from the insurance and risk management field.

Looking to Academia for Consultants

In recent years, corporate research and development expenditures have increased mightily. A perfectly natural and logical development has been for the corporate world to look to qualified academics for research assistance. Insurance companies have looked to insurance academicians for consultants to help solve their problems. To all but the most meticulous minds, such arrangements seem eminently sensible and desirable. A constructive exchange of ideas between the business and academic communities is made possible and the two can help each other.

There appear to be persons both in the industry and in academia who see a problem, even a danger, in this arrangement. They point out that the academic process is not only a teaching function but also a process whereby the subject with which it is entrusted is analyzed, evaluated and, where necessary, criticized and even reformed. These persons ask whether those academicians who are also industry consultants could be objective enough to criticize the industry when necessary. One young academician feels so strongly that he speaks of his fellow academicians who become consultants as "selling their birthright for a mess of pottage."

Exchange is Beneficial

My opinion is that only good can come to both the business and to the academic communities from an exchange of ideas and viewpoints. As for objectivity, in any situation it can be elusive indeed. There are those who sublimate their own viewpoint to another because of the stronger personality of that latter person. At the other extreme, some are as tough as the Islamic judge in the Arabic fable who rendered a judgment that his own hand should be cut off.

Most of us are slotted in between these extremes. An interest, even an economic interest, need not necessarily mitigate against an objective stance. A brilliant, young state legislator recalls the advice of an old, experienced leader of his party. After a warning to vote in accordance with conviction and not to be swayed by lobbyists' arguments, the old pro added, "If you can't drink their liquor and eat their food in the evening and the next day vote against their proposition, you don't belong in the legislature."

19
The Future

The future of risk management depends on two major developments. One is how the speciality itself will evolve internally. The other is how the larger environment of which it is an integral part—in this instance the corporation—will evolve.

The evolution of risk management will depend on how well risk managers use the tools available to achieve the goals that the corporation has set for them. If they choose the best possible solution in handling fortuitous risks, then the speciality will continue to grow. If they do not achieve optimum solutions and some other speciality arises that develops a better approach to the problems of fortuitous risks, then the other speciality will supplant or supersede risk management.

Unstable Corporate Environment

The future of the corporation seems equally cloudy. When evidence of organized dissent by students and civil rights activists was first asserted in the 1960s, one pessimistic academician suggested that the whole risk-sharing process, including insurance, might be in jeopardy. He contended that the risk-sharing process assumes that there is a fairly high degree of stability in the environment in which it operates. If there is too much instability, then the risk-sharing process breaks down completely. There are too many losses to be spread among the persons subject to the loss.

As an example, insurance against the destruction of physical property was completely impractical during the manorial era when the only forms of protection, practically speaking, were a strong castle wall or moat or an efficient army of the lord of the manor.

If the present trend continues, risk managers will rely less on the conventional insurance market either to stabilize or to fund the corporation's fortuitous losses. The most obvious reason for this is that the ability of the conventional insurance market to absorb these risks is not growing as fast as the risks themselves.

Emergence of New Risks

In the late 1960s a severe shortage of insurance capacity for large risks developed. As time went by, this capacity shortage worsened. So the insurance market cut back on accepting fortuitous risks from corporations. In addition, corporations found themselves subjected to a host of new risks for which little or no insurance capacity was available.

These new risks stemmed from the heightened emphasis on product design, with the consequent exposure to product recall and product liability claims. More recently, corporations were finding themselves intensively involved in the problems of hazardous waste disposal, pollution and other environmental problems. Corporate risks involving the perception and proper disposition of socio-economic problems such as concerted action by consumer groups, minority groups, and other activists presented additional hazards.

Corporate Ombudsman

Some students of the corporate environment have said that most large corporations will ultimately have to place on their payrolls, at a high level, an individual who will synthesize all the defensive specialties. This emerging top management official could, in the opinion of some, attain the status of a corporate ombudsman. This official would require enough detachment from the corporation's emphasis on sales, production and similar affirmative specialties, to maintain a fairly objective balance between the short term interest of the corporation and the long range view of what is best for it.

If such an official indeed emerges, it is logical that all of the defensively oriented specialties such as risk management, quality control, auditing, and the like, would ultimately become part of this function.

Throughout this book, much emphasis has been placed on the role which the conventional insurance market plays in handling corporate risks. It is a substantial role. In many instances, it is an expensive solution to corporate problems. Obviously, it is the responsibility of the risk manager to continue to evaluate the economics of using the conventional insurance market to effect what amounts to pooling of that corporation's risks with those of other corporations and individuals subject to the same risk, to see if there is a less expensive way to achieve this pooling.

Government Intervention

Any analysis of the future of risk management must consider the role that government will play in virtually all aspects of life and, in particular, that of the corporation. To the extent that government has injected itself into the insuring process, it is a factor in risk management.

Insurance is a highly regulated industry. Its regulation is justified on the basis that the insurance product ultimately delivered to the consumer must be equitable and not unduly discriminatory. Whatever the merits of that argument, it is a fact that regulatory compliance has certainly added substantially to the cost of the insurance.

This places corporate risk managers in an anomalous position. They believe they do not need regulatory protection. If they did, they wouldn't be risk managers. Yet there is no doubt that the regulatory process is going to continue and increase and that there is no reason to believe that corporate insurance will be exempted.

Quite often a risk manager with huge insurable risks must seek insurance coverage from the insuring mechanisms of the entire free world. This is the only way of attaining sufficient protection. Yet these efforts are often impeded by state insurance laws designed to protect consumers from unscrupulous insurers, not admitted in the state, seeking to exploit uninformed insurance purchasers. Insurance is thus considerably more expensive than it would be without such intensive scrutiny. As a consequence, the insuring mechanism may be pricing itself out of the corporate risk market.

Legislated Coverage

Another aspect of government participation could diminish or even destroy the conventional insurance market. It is the pre-empting by government of whole segments of coverage. For example, the enactment of Medicare has had a far-reaching effect on the life and casualty insurance industry. If Medicare should be broadened into a national health plan, it would undoubtedly change or even supersede workers' compensation, non-work connected disability payment plans, and all plans providing reimbursement for hospital, surgical and similar forms of medical expense.

A national health insurance plan might have a profound effect on auto insurance, rendering moot any argument as to whether auto insurance should be fault or no-fault in nature.

The relative ease with which the government can collect premiums in the form of taxes and insist that the entire group subject to a given risk be covered can often mask the underlying problem but it does not solve the problem.

An example is the government-mandated assigned risk plans or government-sponsored pools to take care of risks which are hard to place. One of the first of these was New York State's assigned risk plan for auto insurance.

My principal objection to this approach is its tendency to bury the problem rather than to solve it. By introducing the assigned risk plan, all automobile owners in New York State who could not otherwise get auto insurance, are able to obtain coverage through the assigned risk plan. Invariably the loss experience of this and similar plans is substantially greater than the loss experience generated by the group not a part of the plan. The rates permitted by the state do not take care of excessive losses, yet insurers have to provide coverage.

Somebody has to pay for these excessive losses. It is the other insurance consumers who ultimately absorb these losses. The state has solved its problem, but the underlying causes, such as a permissive attitude on driver licensing, remain buried.

20
Epilogue

I've had a love affair with the practice of risk management since 1969 when strong willed officers of the insurance managers' professional society said, in effect: "We shall be known as risk managers" and proceeded to provide the leadership to effect that significant change in direction.

Risk management has progressed mightily since then. It has made great progress during the time I have been writing this book. To have observed this progress, along with the conditions and stimuli which prompted it, and to record it in some measure, however small, has been a rare privilege indeed.

"I am loth to close," as Abraham Lincoln once wrote. Before I do I would like to share with you who pursue this practice a little story with a moral to it. It involves Mary, my wife, and the solution to a risk management problem.

Very early in my career as a risk manager, I was called to the office of a top executive of the company for which I worked to evaluate his personal insurance program. All insurance and risk managers perform this task gladly; newly appointed ones even more so.

Somewhat untypical, this gentleman had an automobile about eight years old for which my predecessor had maintained full collision insurance. The maximum he could collect—the "blue book" value of the car—was approximately two and a half times the annual premium for the coverage. The risk/reward ratio was marginal on a gross basis and was even less so on an after-tax basis. The premium had to be paid with after-tax dollars, and if a total loss occurred, much of it could be listed as a casualty loss under the tax code. As an executive of a large corporation, he was at least in a 50 percent tax bracket. So his collision insurance policy was practically worthless to him.

I recommended to him that he drop the coverage. He accepted my recommendation.

Shortly thereafter, my wife Mary suffered a one-car collision accident while driving our new car. She sustained damage approximately equal to the deductible, the highest available at the time. In discussing the repair costs, the rather blunt body shop proprietor, observing that the car was new, asked Mary: "Your insurance will cover this, of course?" To which Mary answered, "No, I don't think so. My husband has a different insurance arrangement." Our blunt "insurance expert" responded: "Your husband is very foolish and doesn't know much about insurance."

That evening Mary, somewhat defensively, told me of the accident. She also reported the body shop proprietor's opinion of my insurance program, with sufficient emphasis to connote her agreement.

With equal defensiveness, I responded: "No doubt your insurance expert is a graduate of the Wharton School with an insurance major, since you accepted his criticism so readily. I'd like you to know that a top executive of the company agreed with me last week on a program of noninsurance on his personal car, even if you don't."

To this Mary responded: "I hope his wife doesn't have an accident." The rest of the evening was spent in chilly silence, a condition which all husbands and wives who know and care and love will understand.

Even after the chill had thawed, I could see that something in this situation was bothering Mary. Only after several months, when I mentioned to her that this gentleman had bought his wife a new car and that I had arranged for the appropriate insurance, including substantial physical damage coverage, did Mary enlighten me by expressing her relief.

She had, instinctively, spotted a "people" problem that I had missed completely. She reasoned that if she and I had gotten into a family argument by virtue of the non-insured arrangement, it was equally possible that the top executive who had agreed to a similar plan, and his wife could have also. And, if that happened, he could well have asked himself: "How good is the insurance advice that I got from Lalley?"

People problems are not usually deduced from reading books on risk management, nor from writing one. Nor from going to the Wharton School. They are learned from knowing and caring for people. That's the lesson I learned from Mary. Risk management is a people business. I shall never forget it. Nor should you.

Finally, to all my friends in risk management, for whom this book has been written with great affection, a final word. For those of you who haven't attained a corporate vice presidency, hang in there! You deserve it! For those of you who have, keep in there! Risk management is good training for the CEO slot. Good-bye for now—good luck and God bless.

Index